Catholic Church Compline

St. Dominic's hymn-book

With the Office of Compline according to the Dominican rite

Catholic Church Compline

St. Dominic's hymn-book
With the Office of Compline according to the Dominican rite

ISBN/EAN: 9783742828606

Manufactured in Europe, USA, Canada, Australia, Japa

Cover: Foto ©Lupo / pixelio.de

Manufactured and distributed by brebook publishing software (www.brebook.com)

Catholic Church Compline

St. Dominic's hymn-book

St. Dominic's Hymn=Book

WITH THE

OFFICE OF COMPLINE

ACCORDING TO THE

DOMINICAN RITE.

BURNS AND OATES.

LONDON:
GRANVILLE MANSIONS,
ORCHARD STREET, W.

NEW YORK:
CATHOLIC PUBLICATION
SOCIETY CO.
BARCLAY STREET.

1885.

Nihil obstat:

    Fr. G. Vincentius King, S.T.M.,
                                  Censor deputatus.

    Fr. Philippus Limerick,
                                  Librorum revisor.

Imprimatur:

    ✠ Henricus Eduardus,
                                  Card. Archiep. Westmon.

Imprimatur:

    Fr. E. Antoninus Williams, O.P.,
                                    Prior Prov. Angl.

Prefatory Note.

The compiler of this little book desires to acknowledge, as taken from *Annus Sanctus*, by kind permission of Orby Shipley, Esq., M.A., the following translations :—

Nos. 9, 11, and 12, by the late Robert Campbell, Esq.; No. 23, by the late R. Campbell, Esq., and J. C. Earle, Esq.; and Nos. 15, 24, 26, 29, 77, 81, and 83 by the late Very Rev. Father Aylward, O.P.

Two hymns—Nos. 45 and 46—appear for the first time.

Sincere thanks are returned for much kind information and assistance received; and should any rights of publication have been unwittingly infringed, earnest apologies are offered.

Contents.

COMPLINE.

	PAGE
THE OFFICE OF COMPLINE ACCORDING TO THE DOMINICAN RITE	11
ANTIPHONS, HYMNS, ETC., PROPER TO VARIOUS SEASONS AND FESTIVALS :—	
CHRISTMAS . . .	23
EPIPHANY . .	24
LENT . .	25
EASTER-DAY	28
PASCHAL TIME . . .	29
ASCENSION	30
WHITSUN-DAY . .	31
CORPUS CHRISTI	31
FEASTS OF THE B. V. MARY . .	32

CONTENTS.

HYMNS, ETC.

Advent.

No.
1. Hark, an awful voice is sounding . . . . . *tr. Caswall.*
2. Dear Maker of the starry skies . . . . . . *tr. Caswall.*
3. Like the dawning of the morning . . . . . . *Faber.*

Christmas.

4. Angels we have heard on high . . . .
5. Adeste, fidéles . . . .
6. Ye faithful, approach ye . . . . *tr. Oakeley.*
7. See, amid the winter's snow . . . . *Caswall.*
8. Stars of glory, shine more brightly . . . . *Husenbeth.*

Epiphany and Holy Name.

9. What beauteous sun-surpassing star . . . *tr. Campbell.*
10. Jesus, the only thought of thee . *tr. from St. Bernard.*

Lent.

11. O gracious Lord, Creator dear . . . . . *tr. Campbell.*
12. Again the time appointed see . . . . . *tr. Campbell.*
13. Now are the days of humblest prayer . . . . . *Faber.*
14. Miserere mei, Deus . . . . *Psalm 50.*

Passion-Tide.

15. Stabat Mater dolorosa — Weeping sore, the Mother stood . . . . . } . . *tr. Aylward.*
16. O'erwhelmed in depths of woe . . . . . . *tr. Caswall.*
17. Oh, come and mourn with me awhile . . . . . *Faber.*
18. My Jesus, say, what wretch has dared . . . . } *tr. from St. Alphonsus.*
19. What a sea of tears and sorrow . . . . . *tr. Caswall.*

Easter.

20. The dawn was purpling o'er the sky . . . . *tr. Caswall.*
21. Ye sons and daughters of the Lord . . . . *tr. Caswall.*
22. All hail, dear Conqueror, all hail . . . . *Faber*

Ascension.

No.
23. Thy sacred race, O Lord, is run . *tr. Campbell and Earle.*

Whitsun-Tide.

24. Holy Spirit, come and shine . . . . . . *tr. Aylward.*
25. Veni, Creator Spiritus . . . .
26. Creator-Spirit, all-divine . . . . *tr. Aylward.*
27. Holy Ghost, come down upon thy children . . . . *Faber.*

Trinity Sunday.

28. Have mercy on us, God most high . . . . . . *Faber.*

Corpus Christi.

29. Pange lingua gloriosi corporis—Sing, my joyful tongue, the mystery . . . *tr. Aylward.*
30. Jesus, my Lord, my God, my all . . . . *Faber.*
31. When the Patriarch was returning . . . . *tr. Caswall.*

Sacred Heart of Jesus.

32. To Christ, the Prince of peace . . . . . . *tr. Caswall.*
33. To Jesus' Heart, all burning . . . . . . *tr. Christie.*

The Precious Blood.

34. Hail, Jesus, hail, who for my sake . . . . *Faber.*

Feasts of the Blessed Virgin.

35. Ave maria stella—Hail, thou Star of ocean . *tr. Aylward.*
36. Daily, daily, sing to Mary . . . *Birmingham Oratory.*
37. Hail, Queen of heaven, the ocean star . . . . *Lingard.*
38. Look down, O Mother Mary . . *tr. from St. Alphonsus.*
39. Mother of mercy, day by day . . . . *Faber.*

CONTENTS. vii

Immaculate Conception.

No.
40. O purest of creatures, sweet Mother, sweet Maid . *Faber.*
41. O Mother! I could weep for mirth . . . . . . *Faber.*

Assumption.

42. Sing, sing, ye Angel bands . . . . *Faber.*

Month of Mary.

43. Joy of my heart! oh let me pay . . . . . . *Faber.*
44. This is the image of our Queen . . . . . . *Caswall.*

Holy Rosary.

45. The clouds hang thick o'er Israel's camp . *A. T. Drane.*
46. Queen of the Holy Rosary . . . . *E. M. S.*
47. Hail, full of grace.—Joyful mysteries . . . *P. F. C.*
48. Lord, by thy prayer.—Sorrowful mysteries . . *P. F. C.*
49. All hail, great Conqueror.—Glorious mysteries *P. F. C.*

Guardian Angel.

50. Dear Angel, ever at my side . . . . *Faber.*

St. Joseph.

51. Hail! holy Joseph, hail . . . . *Faber.*
52. Dear Husband of Mary! dear Nurse of her Child. *Faber.*

SS. Peter and Paul.

53. It is no earthly summer's ray . . . . . . *tr. Faber.*

St. Dominic.

54. Sound the mighty champion's praises . . . *tr. Aylward.*
55. Thou who, hero-like, hast striven . . . . *A. T. Drane.*

St. George.

No.
56. O thou, of all thy warriors Lord . . . . *tr. Caswall.*

St. Patrick.

57. Hail, glorious Saint Patrick . . . .

St. Thomas Aquinas.

58. Flower of innocence, Saint Thomas . . . . *P. F. C.*

St. Mary Magdalen.

59. Once a very sinful woman . . . . *Greene*

St. Catherine of Siena.

60. O spouse of Christ, on whom . . . . . . *A. T. Drane.*

All Saints.

61. O Christ, thy guilty people spare . . . . . *tr. Caswall.*

All Souls.

62. De profundis clamávi ad te . . . . *Psalm* 129.
63. Oh, turn to Jesus, Mother, turn . . . . . . *Faber.*

Missions and Retreats.

64. Hail, holy Mission, hail . . . . *Chadwick.*
65. Oh, come to the merciful Saviour that calls you . *Faber.*
66. Jesus, my God, behold at length the time . . *Chadwick.*
67. God of mercy and compassion . . . . . . *Vaughan.*

CONTENTS.

Occasional.

No.
68. My God, how wonderful thou art . . . . *Faber.*
69. I worship thee, sweet Will of God . . . . . . *Faber.*
70. My God, I love thee, not because . . . . *tr. Caswall.*
71. Jesus is God; the solid earth . . . . *Faber.*
72. O Jesus, Jesus, dearest Lord . . . . *Faber.*
73. Hark, hark, my soul, angelic songs are swelling . . *Faber.*
74. O Paradise! O Paradise . . . . *Faber.*
75. Hark! the sound of the fight hath gone forth . . *Faber.*
76. Faith of our Fathers! living still . . . . . . *Faber.*

Evening.

77. O Christ, thou brightness of the day . . . *tr. Aylward.*
78. Sweet Saviour, bless us ere we go . . . . . . *Faber.*

Benediction of the Most Holy Sacrament.

79. O salutaris hostia—O saving Victim . . . *tr. Caswall.*
80. Litany of the Blessed Virgin . . . .
81. Tantum ergo Sacramentum—Wherefore this dread Host adoring . . . } . . *tr. Aylward.*
82. Adoremus in æternum . . . .
83. Adoro te devote, latens Deitas—Thee prostrate I adore, the Deity that lies . . . . } . . *tr. Aylward.*
84. Ave verum Corpus natum—Hail to thee! true Body, sprung . . . . } . . *tr. Caswall.*
85. Inviolata, intacta, et casta es—Spotless and pure, Mary immaculate . } . . *tr. P. F. C.*
86. Te Deum laudamus . . . .

---

87. Litany of the Holy Name of Jesus.

PRAYER BEFORE COMPLINE.

O SACRUM convívium, in quo Christus súmitur! recólitur memória passiónis ejus: mens implétur grátia: et futuræ glóriæ nobis pignus datur.
V. Panem de cœlo præstitísti eis.
R. Omne delectaméntum in se habéntem.

OREMUS.

DEUS, qui nobis sub Sacraménto mirábili Passiónis tuæ memóriam reliquísti; tríbue, quæsumus, ita nos Córporis et Sánguinis tui sacra mystéria venerári, ut redemptiónis tuæ fructum in nobis júgiter sentiámus. Qui vivis et regnas in sæcula sæculórum. R. Amen.

Dómine in unióne illíus divinæ intentiónis, qua ipse in terris laudes Deo persolvísti, has tibi horas persólvo.

O SACRED banquet, wherein Christ is received, the memory of his Passion is renewed, the soul is filled with grace, and a pledge of future glory is given to us.
V. Thou didst give them bread from heaven.
R. Containing in itself all sweetness.

LET US PRAY.

O GOD, who in this wonderful Sacrament has left us a memorial of thy Passion; grant us, we beseech thee, so to reverence the sacred mysteries of thy Body and Blood, that we may continually feel in our souls the fruit of thy redemption. Who livest and reignest for ever and ever. R. Amen.

O Lord, in union with that divine intention wherewith thou didst when on earth praise God, I offer these prayers to thee.

PRAYER AFTER COMPLINE.

SACROSÁNCTÆ et indivíduæ Trinitáti, crucifíxi Dómini nostri Jesu Christi humanitáti, beatíssimæ et gloriosíssimæ sempérque Vírginis Maríæ fecúndæ integritáti et ómnium Sanctórum universitáti sit sempitérna laus, honor, virtus, et glória ab omni creatúra; nobísque remíssio ómnium peccatórum, per infiníta sæcula sæculórum. Amen.

V. Beáta viscera Maríæ Vírginis, quæ portavérunt ætérni Patris Fílium.
R. Et beáta úbera quæ lactavérunt Christum Dóminum.

Pater noster. Ave Maria.

TO the most holy and undivided Trinity, to the humanity of our Lord Jesus Christ crucified, to the fruitful virginity of the most blessed and glorious Mary ever Virgin, and to the whole company of saints, be for ever praise, honour, power, and glory from every creature; and to us be remission of all sins, world without end. Amen.

V. Blessed is the womb of Mary the Virgin, which bore the Son of the Eternal Father.
R. And blessed are the breasts which gave suck to Christ the Lord.

Our Father. Hail Mary.

COMPLINE.

At the beginning of Compline the people stand.

JUBE domne, benedícere.

PRAY, Father, give the blessing.

THE BLESSING.

NOCTEM quiétam, et finem perféctum tríbuat nobis omnípotens et miséricors Dóminus. R. Amen.

MAY the Almighty and merciful Lord grant us a quiet night, and perfect end. R. Amen.

SHORT LESSON. 1 Peter v. 8.

FRATRES, sóbrii estóte, et vigiláte: quia adversárius vester diábolus tamquam leo rúgiens círcuit, quærens quem dévoret: cui resístite, fortes in fide. Tu autem, Dómine, miserére nostri.
R. Deo grátias.
V. Adjutórium nostrum in nómine Dómini. R. Qui fecit cœlum et terram.

Pater noster, *secreto.*
Priest. Confíteor, etc.
Choir. Misereátur tui om-

BRETHREN, be sober and watch: because your adversary the devil, as a roaring lion, goeth about, seeking whom he may devour; whom resist ye, strong in faith. But do thou, O Lord, have mercy on us.
R. Thanks be to God.
V. Our help is in the name of the Lord. R. Who hath made heaven and earth.
Our Father, *in silence.*
Priest. I confess, etc.
Choir. May Almighty God

nípotens Deus, et dimíttat tibi ómnia peccáta tua, líberet te ab omni malo ; salvet et confírmet in omni ópere bono, et perdúcat te ad vitam ætérnam.

Priest. Amen.
Choir. Confíteor Deo omnipoténti, et beátæ Maríæ semper Vírgini, et beáto Domínico Patri nostro, et ómnibus Sanctis, et tibi, Pater, quia peccávi nimis cogitátione, locútione, ópere, et omissióne, mea culpa : precor te oráre pro me.

Priest. Misereatur, etc.

V. Convérte nos, Deus salutáris noster. R. Et avérte iram tuam a nobis.
V. Deus, in adjutórium meum inténde. R. Dómine, ✠ ad adjuvándum me festína.
Glória Patri, et Fílio, et Spirítui sancto. Sicut erat in princípio, et nunc, et semper, et in saécula sæculórum. Amen.

Alleluia.

have mercy on thee, and forgive thee all thy sins, deliver thee from every evil ; preserve and strengthen thee in every good work, and bring thee to life everlasting.

Priest. Amen.
Choir. I confess to Almighty God, to Blessed Mary ever Virgin, to Blessed Dominic our Father, to all Saints, and to thee, Father : that I have sinned exceedingly in thought, word, deed, and omission, through my fault : I beseech thee to pray for me.

Priest. May Almighty God, etc.

V. Convert us, O God, our Saviour. R. And turn away thy anger from us.
V. O God, come to my assistance. R. O Lord, make haste to help me.

Glory be to the Father, and to the Son, and to the Holy Ghost. As it was in the beginning, is now, and ever shall be, world without end. Amen.

Alleluia.

From Septuagesima until the end of Lent instead of Alleluia *is said :*

Laus tibi, Dómine, Rex ætérnæ glóriæ.
Antiphon. Miserére.

Praise be to thee, O Lord, King of eternal glory.
Have mercy.

The people sit during the Psalms.

PSALM IV.

CUM invocárem exaudívit me Deus justítiæ meæ : * in tribulatióne dilatásti mihi.

2. Miserére mei : * et exaúdi oratiónem meam.
3. Fílii hóminum úsquequo gravi corde : * ut quid dilígitis vanitátem, et quæritis mendácium ?
4. Et scitóte quóniam mirificávit Dóminus sanctum suum : * Dóminus exaúdiet me, cum clamávero ad eum.
5. Irascímini, et nolíte peccáre : * quæ dícitis in córdibus vestris, in cubílibus vestris compungímini.
6. Sacrificáte sacrifícium justítiæ, ¿ et speráte in Dómino : * multi dicunt : quis osténdit nobis bona ?
7. Signátum est super nos lumen vultus tui Dómine : * dedísti lætítiam in corde meo.
8. A fructu fruménti, vini, et ólei sui : * multiplicáti sunt.
9. In pace in idípsum : * dórmiam, et requiéscam.
10. Quóniam tu, Dómine, singuláriter in spe : * constituísti me.

Glória Patri et Fílio : * et Spirítui sancto.
Sicut erat in princípio, et

WHEN I called upon him, the God of my justice heard me : when I was in distress thou hast enlarged me.
Have mercy on me : and hear my prayer.
O ye sons of men, how long will ye be dull of heart : why do you love vanity and seek after lying ?
Know ye also that the Lord hath made his Holy One wonderful : the Lord will hear me, when I shall cry unto him.
Be ye angry, and sin not : the things you say in your hearts, be sorry for them upon your beds.
Offer up the sacrifice of justice, and trust in the Lord : many say : Who showeth us good things ?
The light of thy countenance, O Lord, is signed upon us : thou hast given gladness in my heart.
By the fruit of their corn, their wine and oil : they are multiplied.
In peace in the selfsame : I will sleep and I will rest.
For thou, O Lord : singularly hast settled me in hope.

Glory be to the Father and to the Son : and to the Holy Ghost. As it was in

nunc et semper: * et in saécula sæculórum. Amen.

the beginning, is now, and ever shall be, world without end. Amen.

PSALM XXX.

IN te Dómine sperávi, non confúndar in ætérnum: * in justítia tua líbera me.

2. Inclína ad me aurem tuam: * accélera ut éruas me.
3. Esto mihi in Deum protectórem, et in domum refúgii: * ut salvum me fácias.
4. Quóniam fortitúdo mea, et refúgium meum es tu: * et propter nomen tuum dedúces me, et enútries me.
5. Edúces me de láqueo hoc, quem abscondérunt mihi: * quóniam tu es protéctor meus.
6. In manus tuas comméndo spíritum meum: * redemísti me, Dómine Deus veritátis.

Glória Patri et Fílio: * et Spirítui sancto.

Sicut erat in princípio, et nunc, et semper: * et in saécula sæculórum. Amen.

IN thee, O Lord, have I hoped, let me never be confounded: deliver me in thy justice.

Bow down thy ear to me: make haste to deliver me.

Be thou unto me a God, a protector, and a house of refuge: to save me.

For thou art my strength and my refuge: and for thy name's sake thou wilt lead me and nourish me.

Thou wilt bring me out of this snare which they have hidden for me: for thou art my protector.

Into thy hands I commend my spirit: thou hast redeemed me, O Lord, the God of truth.

Glory be to the Father and to the Son: and to the Holy Ghost. As it was in the beginning, is now, and ever shall be, world without end. Amen.

PSALM XC.

In Easter Week (see page 28) and Whitsun Week this Psalm is omitted.

QUI hábitat in adjutório Altíssimi: * in protectióne Dei cœli commorábitur.

HE that dwelleth in the aid of the Most High: shall abide under the protection of the God of heaven.

COMPLINE. 15

2. Dicet Dómino: suscéptor meus es tu, et refúgium meum: * Deus meus, sperábo in eum.
3. Quóniam ipse liberávit me de láqueo venántium: * et a verbo áspero.
4. Scápulis suis obumbrábit tibi: * et sub pennis ejus sperábis.
5. Scuto circúmdabit te véritas ejus: * non timébis a timóre noctúrno.
6. A sagítta volánte in die, ⸸ a negótio perambulánte in ténebris: * ab incúrsu, et dæmónio meridiáno.
7. Cadent a látere tuo mille, ⸸ et decem míllia a dextris tuis: * ad te autem non appropinquábit.
8. Verúmtamen óculis tuis considerábis: * et retributiónem peccatórum vidébis.
9. Quóniam tu es, Dómine, spes mea: * Altíssimum posuísti refúgium tuum.
10. Non accédet ad te malum: * et flagéllum non appropinquábit tabernáculo tuo.
11. Quóniam Angelis suis mandávit de te: * ut custódiant te in ómnibus viis tuis.

He shall say to the Lord: Thou art my protector and my refuge: my God, in him will I trust.

For he hath delivered me from the snare of the hunters: and from the sharp sword.

He will overshadow thee with his shoulders: and under his wing thou shalt trust.

His truth shall compass thee with a shield: thou shalt not be afraid of the terror of the night.

Of the arrow that flieth in the day, of the business that walketh about in the dark: of invasion, and of the noonday devil.

A thousand shall fall at thy side, and ten thousand at thy right hand: but the evil shall not come nigh thee.

But thou shalt consider with thy eyes: and shalt see the reward of the wicked.

Because thou, O Lord, art my hope: thou hast made the Most High thy refuge.

There shall no evil come to thee: nor shall the scourge come near thy dwelling.

For he hath given his angels charge over thee: to keep thee in all thy ways.

12. In mánibus portábunt te : * ne forte offéndas ad lápidem pedem tuum.
13. Super áspidem, et basilíscum ambulábis : * et conculcábis leónem et dracónem.
14. Quóniam in me sperávit, liberábo eum : * prótegam eum, quóniam cognóvit nomen meum.
15. Clamábit ad me, et ego exaúdiam eum : cum ipso sum in tribulatióne : * erípiam eum, et glorificábo eum.
16. Longitúdine diérum replébo eum : * et osténdam illi salutáre meum.
Glória Patri et Fílio : * et Spirítui sancto.
Sicut erat in princípio, et nunc, et semper: * et in saécula sæculórum. Amen.

In their hands they shall bear thee up : lest thou dash thy foot against a stone.
Thou shalt walk upon the asp and the basilisk : and thou shalt trample under foot the lion and the dragon.
Because he hoped in me, I will deliver him : I will protect him, because he hath known my name.
He shall cry to me, and I will hear him : I am with him in tribulation : I will deliver him, and will glorify him.
I will fill him with length of days : and I will show him my salvation.
Glory be to the Father and to the Son : and to the Holy Ghost. As it was in the beginning, is now, and ever shall be, world without end. Amen.

PSALM CXXXIII.

ECCE nunc benedicite Dóminum : * omnes servi Dómini.
2. Qui statis in domo Dómini : * in átriis domus Dei nostri.
3. In nóctibus extóllite manus vestras in sancta : * et benedícite Dóminum.
4. Benedícat te Dóminus ex Sion : * qui fecit cœlum et terram.
Glória Patri et Fílio : * et Spirítui sancto.

BEHOLD now bless ye the Lord : all ye servants of the Lord :
Who stand in the house of the Lord : in the courts of the house of our God.
In the nights lift up your hands to the holy places : and bless ye the Lord.
May the Lord out of Sion bless thee : he that made heaven and earth.
Glory be to the Father and to the Son : and to the

COMPLINE. 17

Sicut erat in princípio, et nunc, et semper : * et in saécula sæculórum. Amen.

Antiphon. Miserére mei Dómine, et exaúdi oratiónem meam.

Antiphon in Paschal time. Allelúia, allelúia, allelúia, allelúia.

Holy Ghost. As it was in the beginning, is now, and ever shall be, world without end. Amen.

Have mercy on me, O Lord, and graciously hear my prayer.

Here the people rise, and remain standing until the Blessing.

LITTLE CHAPTER. Jer. xiv. 9.

TU in nobis es, Dómine, et nomen sanctum tuum invocátum est super nos : ne derelínquas nos, Dómine Deus noster.
R. Deo grátias.

THOU, O Lord, art among us, and thy holy name is invoked upon us : forsake us not, O Lord our God.
R. Thanks be to God.

RESPONSORY.

From the first Sunday of Lent until the eve of Passion Sunday, see page 25.

IN manus tuas, Dómine, comméndo spíritum meum.
In manus tuas, etc.
V. Redemísti me, Dómine, Deus veritátis.
Comméndo spíritum meum.
V. Glória Patri, et Fílio, et Spirítui sancto.
In manus tuas, Dómine, comméndo spíritum meum.

INTO thy hands, O Lord, I commend my spirit.
Into thy hands, etc.
V. Thou hast redeemed me, O Lord, the God of truth.
I commend my spirit.
V. Glory be to the Father, and to the Son, etc.
Into thy hands, O Lord, I commend my spirit.

On greater doubles, within solemn octaves, and in Paschal time, the Responsory is said as follows:

COMPLINE.

IN manus tuas, Dómine, comméndo spíritum meum. Allelúia, allelúia.
In manus tuas, etc.
V. Redemísti me, Dómine, Deus veritátis.

Allelúia, allelúia.
V. Glória Patri et Fílio: et Spirítui sancto.
In manus tuas, Dómine, comméndo spíritum meum. Allelúia, allelúia.

INTO thy hands, O Lord, I commend my spirit. Alleluia, alleluia.
Into thy hands, etc.
V. Thou hast redeemed me, O Lord, the God of truth.
Alleluia, alleluia.
V. Glory be to the Father and to the Son, etc.
Into thy hands, O Lord, I commend my spirit. Alleluia, alleluia.

HYMN.

In Lent see page 25, and in Paschal time, page 29.

TE lucis ante términum,
  Rerum creátor, póscimus,
Ut sólita cleméntia
Sis præsul ad custódiam.

Procul recédant sómnia
Et nóctium phantásmata;
Hostémque nostrum cómprime
Ne polluántur córpora.

BEFORE the closing of
  the day,   [pray,
Creator, thee we humbly
That, for thy wonted mercy's
  sake,   [take.
Thou us into protection

May nothing in our minds
  excite   [of the night;
Vain dreams and phantoms
Our enemy repress, that so
Our bodies no uncleanness
  know.

[*On Feasts of our Lady, next verse* Maria mater gratiæ.]

Præsta, Pater omnípotens,
Per Jesum Christum Dominum,
Qui tecum in perpétuum,
Regnat cum sancto Spíritu.
                    Amen.

Almighty Father, this accord   [Son, our Lord;
Through Jesus Christ thy
Who, with the Holy Ghost
  and thee
Doth live and reign eternally. Amen.

This last verse varies on certain days (see pages 23, 24, 31); and on Feasts of our Lady the two following verses are sung in its place:

María, mater grátiæ,
Mater misericórdiæ,
Tu nos ab hoste prótege,
Et hora mortis súscipe.

Glória tibi, Dómine,
Qui natus es de Vírgine,
Cum Patre et sancto Spíritu,
In sempitérna sæcula.
    Amen.

V. Custódi nos, Dómine,
ut pupíllam óculi.
R. Sub umbra alárum
tuárum prótege nos.
Antiphon. Salva nos.

O Mary, mother of all grace
And mercy to our sinful
  race,   [power,
Protect us from the demon's
And take us at life's closing
  hour.

All glory be to thee, O Lord,
A Virgin's Son, o'er all
  adored,   [greet
And equal praise for ever
The Father and the Paraclete. Amen.

V. Keep us, O Lord, as
the apple of thine eye.
R. Protect us under the
shadow of thy wings.
Save us.

NUNC DIMITTIS. S. Luke ii.

NUNC dimíttis servum
  tuum, Dómine : * secúndum verbum tuum in pace.
  Quia vidérunt óculi mei : * salutáre tuum.
  Quod parásti : * ante fáciem ómnium populórum.

Lumen ad revelatiónem gentium : * et gloriam plebis tuæ Israel.
  Gloria Patri et Fílio : * et Spirítui sancto.
  Sicut erat in princípio, et nunc, et semper : * et in sæcula sæculorum. Amen.

Antiphon. Salva nos, Dómine, vigilántes, custódi nos dormiéntes : ut vigilémus

NOW dost thou dismiss
  thy servant, O Lord,
in peace : according to thy
  word.
  For mine eyes have seen :
thy salvation.
  Which thou hast prepared : before the face of all
  people :
  A light to enlighten the
Gentiles : and the glory of
thy people Israel.
  Glory be to the Father, and
to the Son : and to the Holy
Ghost. As it was in the
beginning, is now, and ever
shall be : world without
end. Amen.
  Save us, O Lord, when
we are awake, and keep us
while we sleep : that we

cum Christo, et requiescámus in pace.
V. Dóminus vobíscum.
R. Et cum spíritu tuo.
OREMUS.

VISITA, quæsumus Dómine, habitatiónem istam, et omnes insídias inimíci ab ea longe repélle : et Angeli tui sancti habitántes in ea, nos in pace custódiant, et benedíctio tua sit super nos semper. Per Dóminum.
R. Amen.
V. Dóminus vobíscum.
R. Et cum spíritu tuo.
V. Benedicámus Dómino.
R. Deo grátias.

may watch with Christ, and rest in peace.
V. The Lord be with you.
R. And with thy spirit.
LET US PRAY.

VISIT, we beseech thee, O Lord, this habitation, and drive far from it all snares of the enemy: let thy holy angels dwell herein, to keep us in peace : and may thy blessing be always upon us. Through our Lord, etc. R. Amen.
V. The Lord be with you.
R. And with thy spirit.
V. Let us bless the Lord.
R. Thanks be to God.

Here the people kneel.

BENEDICTIO Dei omnipoténtis Patris, ✠ et Fílii, et Spíritus sancti, descéndat super nos et máneat semper. R. Amen.

MAY the blessing of Almighty God, Father, Son, and Holy Ghost, descend upon us and remain with us always. R. Amen.

THE PROCESSION.

NOTE.—For greater solemnity and devotion, the following Antiphon to the Blessed Virgin is sung in procession, and during it the priest blesses those present with holy water. This procession has been customary in all Dominican churches since the year 1226, when it was instituted by Blessed Jordan of Saxony, the immediate successor of St. Dominic in the government of his Order. Pope Paul V. granted an indulgence of 200 days to all the faithful each time they should assist at it.

SALVE, Regína, Mater misericórdiæ,
Vita, dulcédo, et spes nostra salve,
Ad te clamámus, éxules filii Evæ.

HAIL, holy Queen, Mother of mercy,
Hail, our life, our sweetness, and our hope.
To thee do we cry, poor banished children of Eve.

COMPLINE. 21

Ad te suspirámus geméntes et flentes in hac lacrymárum valle.

Eia ergo, advocáta nostra, illos tuos misericórdes óculos ad nos convérte.

Et Jesum, benedíctum fructum ventris tui, nobis post hoc exílium osténde.

O clemens,
O pia,
O dulcis Virgo Maria.

To thee do we send up our sighs, mourning and weeping in this vale of tears.

Turn, then, most gracious advocate, thine eyes of mercy towards us.

And after this our exile, shew unto us the blessed fruit of thy womb, Jesus.

O clement,
O loving.
O sweet Virgin Mary.

In Paschal time, Alleluia.

V. Dignáre me laudáre te, Virgo sacráta.
R. Da mihi virtútem contra hostes tuos.

V. Vouchsafe that I may praise thee, O sacred Virgin.
R. Give me strength against thine enemies.

OREMUS.

CONCEDE nos fámulos tuos, quaésumus, Dómine Deus, perpétua mentis et córporis salúte gaudére, et gloriósa beátæ Maríæ semper Vírginis intercessióne, a presénti liberári tristítia, et ætérna pérfrui lætítia. Per Christum Dóminum nostrum. *R.* Amen.

LET US PRAY.

GRANT to us thy servants, we beseech thee, O Lord God, to enjoy perpetual health of mind and body, and, by the glorious intercession of blessed Mary ever Virgin, to be delivered from present sorrow and to enjoy eternal gladness. Through, etc. *R.* Amen.

Then, as the procession returns, is sung this Antiphon to St. Dominic.

O LUMEN Ecclésiæ,
Doctor veritátis,
Rosa patiéntiæ,
Ebur castitátis.

O LIGHT of holy Church,
Teacher of truth divine!
Sweet rose of patience, ivory white
Thy chastity doth shine.

Aquam sapiéntiæ
Propinásti gratis;
Prædicátor grátiæ,
Nos junge beátis.

Of wisdom's living waters
All freely thou hast given:
O messenger of grace to men,
Lift thou our souls to heaven.

In Paschal time, Alleluia.

V. Ora pro nobis, beáte Pater Domínice.
R. Ut digni efficiámur promissiónibus Christi.

V. Pray for us, O holy Father St. Dominic.
R. That we may be made worthy of the promises of Christ.

OREMUS.

CONCEDE, quæsumus, omnípotens Deus: ut qui peccatórum nostrórum póndere prémimur, beati Domínici Confessóris tui, Patris nostri, patrocínio sublevémur. Per Christum Dóminum nostrum.

R. Amen.

Fidélium ánimæ per misericórdiam Dei requiéscant in pace.
R. Amen.

Pater noster. Credo.

LET US PRAY.

GRANT, we beseech thee, Almighty God, that we who are weighed down by the burden of our sins may be relieved by the intercession of the blessed Dominic, thy Confessor and our Father. Through Christ our Lord.
R. Amen.

May the souls of the faithful through the mercy of God rest in peace.
R. Amen.

Our Father. I believe.

ANTIPHONS, HYMNS, ETC.,
FOR VARIOUS SEASONS.

The following Antiphons are appointed to be used after the Psalms and Nunc dimittis in place of the ordinary ones beginning Miserere and Salva nos respectively.

CHRISTMAS-EVE.

After the Psalms.

COMPLETI sunt dies Maríæ, ut páreret Fílium suum primogénitum.

THE days of Mary were fulfilled, that she should bring forth her first-born Son.

After Nunc dimittis.

Ecce complétasunt ómnia, quæ dicta sunt per Angelum de Vírgine María.

Behold all things were accomplished, which were said by the Angel, of the Virgin Mary.

CHRISTMAS-DAY, AND UNTIL THE EVE OF THE EPIPHANY.

After the Psalms.

NATUS est nobis hódie Salvátor, qui est Christus Dóminus, in civitáte David.

TO-DAY is born to us a Saviour, who is Christ the Lord, in the city of David.

After Nunc dimittis.

Allelúia. Verbum caro factum est, allelúia : et habitávit in nobis, allelúia, allelúia.

Alleluia. The Word was made flesh, alleluia : and dwelt amongst us, alleluia, alleluia.

From Christmas-eve until the Eve of the Epiphany the third verse of the hymn Te lucis ante terminum *is sung thus:*

Glória tibi, Dómine,
Qui natus es de Vírgine,
Cum Patre et sancto Spíritu,
In sempitérna sæcula.
Amen.

All glory be to thee, O Lord,
A Virgin's Son, o'er all adored, [greet,
And equal praise for ever
The Father and the Paraclete. Amen.

EPIPHANY, AND DURING THE OCTAVE.

After the Psalms.

LUX de luce apparuísti, Christe, cui Magi múnera ófferunt, allelúia, allelúia, allelúia.

THOU, O Christ, Light of light, hast appeared, to whom the Magi offered gifts, alleluia, alleluia, alleluia.

After Nunc dimittis.

Allelúia. Omnes de Saba vénient, allelúia : aurum et thus deferéntes, allelúia, allelúia.

Alleluia. All shall come from Saba, alleluia : bringing gold and frankincense, alleluia, alleluia.

At the same time the third verse of the hymn Te lucis ante terminum *is sung thus:*

Glória tibi, Dómine,
Qui apparuísti hódie,
Cum Patre et sancto Spíritu,
In sempitérna sæcula.
Amen.

All glory, Lord, to thee we pay, [shines to-day ;
Whose light so brightly
All glory, as is ever meet,
To Father and to Paraclete. Amen.

Sunday within the Octave of the Epiphany is the feast of the FINDING OF OUR LORD IN THE TEMPLE,[*] *when the Antiphons are as follows:*

After the Psalms.

INVENERUNT Jesum paréntes ejus in templo sedéntem in médio doctórum.

HIS parents found Jesus in the temple, sitting in the midst of the doctors.

After Nunc dimittis.

Allelúia. Stupébant omnes, qui eum audiébant, allelúia : super prudéntia et respónsis ejus, allelúia, allelúia.

Alleluia. All that heard him were astonished, alleluia : at his wisdom and answers, alleluia, alleluia.

And the third verse of the hymn is sung thus:

Jesu, tibi sit gloria,
Qui te revélas ánxiis,
Cum Patre et almo Spiritu
In sempiterna sæcula.
Amen.

Jesu, be glory thine, who art
The light that cheers the anxious heart ;
Be glory, as is ever meet,
To Father and to Paraclete. Amen.

[*] When the Epiphany falls on Sunday, this festival is kept on the following Wednesday.

COMPLINE.

LENT, BEGINNING FROM THE FIRST SUNDAY.

RESPONSORY.

Sung in place of In manus tuas, Domine, *until the Eve of Passion Sunday.*

IN pace, in idípsum, dórmiam et requiéscam.
V. Si dédero somnum óculis meis et pálpebris meis dormitatiónem.
Dórmiam et requiéscam.
Glória Patri et Filio, et Spíritui sancto.
In pace, in idípsum, dórmiam et requiéscam.

IN peace, in the selfsame, I will sleep and rest.
If I should give peace to my eyes and slumber to my eyelids.
I will sleep and rest.
Glory be to the Father, and to the Son, etc.
In peace, in the selfsame, I will sleep and rest.

HYMN.

In place of Te lucis ante terminum *until Maundy Thursday.*

CHRISTE, qui lux es et dies,
Noctis tenébras détegia,
Lucísque lumen créderis,
Lumen beátum prædicans.

CHRIST of our souls the noonday bright,
All darkness flies before thy ray; [light,
We own thee very Light of That teileth of the blissful day.

Precámur, sancte Dómine,
Defénde nos in hac nocte;
Sit nobis in te réquies,
Quiétam noctem tríbue.

Most holy Lord, we pray thee then,
Throughout this night our guardian be; [pose
Grant to us now to find re-
And our eternal rest in thee.

Ne gravis somnus írruat,
Nec hostis nos subrípiat,
Nec caro illi conséntiens
Nos tibi reos státuat.

Let us not sleep the sleep of death, [prise;
Nor any foe our souls sur-
Lest evil promptings win consent, [eyes.
And find us guilty in thine

B

Oculi somnum cápiant,
Cor ad te semper vígilet:
Déxtera tua prótegat
Fámulos, qui te díligunt.

Defénsor noster, áspice,
Iusidiántes réprime :
Gubérna tuos fámulos,
Quos sánguine mercátus es.
[*Kneel at last line.*]

Meménto nostri, Dómine,
In gravi isto córpore :
Qui es defénsor ánimæ,
Adésto nobis, Dómine.

Præsta, Pater omnípotens,
Per Jesum Christum Dominum,
Qui tecum in perpétuum
Regnat cum sancto Spíritu.
Amen.

V. Custódi nos, Dómine,
ut pupíllam óculi.
R. Sub umbra alárum
tuárum prótege nos.

Though sleep our eyelids
close, our hearts
Shall ever watch, O Lord,
to thee ; [thy hand
Who love thee well, beneath
Shall rest in sweet security.

Look on us, Lord ; in thee
we trust
To crush the tempter's
every scheme ;
Thy servants guide and rule,
whom thou
Didst with thy precious
blood redeem.

Be mindful of us, Lord, the
while [we bear ;
This burden of the flesh
Defender of the soul, vouchsafe [presence near.
Our souls may find thy

Almighty Father, hear our
cry, [whom all adore ;
Through Jesus Christ,
Who in the Spirit's unity,
Reigneth with thee for
evermore. Amen.

V. Keep us, O Lord, as
the apple of thine eye.
R. Protect us under the
shadow of thy wings.

Then Nunc dimittis (*page* 19), *with one of the following antiphons, according to the time.*

ANTIPHONS AFTER *NUNC DIMITTIS.*

I. *For the first and second weeks of Lent.*

EVIGILA super nos, ætérne Salvátor, ne nos apprehéndat cállidus tentátor, quia tu factus es nobis sempitérnus adjutor.

WATCH over us, O everlasting Redeemer, lest we be ensnared by the wily tempter, for thou art our never-failing helper.

II. *For the third and fourth weeks.*

MEDIA vita in morte sumus: quem quaérimus adjutórem, nisi te, Dómine? qui pro peccátis nostris juste irásceris: Sancte Deus, Sancte fortis, Sancte et miséricors Salvátor, amáræ morti ne tradas nos.

V. Ne projícias nos in témpore senectútis: cum defécerit virtus nostra, ne derelínquas nos, Dómine.

Sancte Deus, Sancte fortis, Sancte et miséricors Salvátor, amáræ morti ne tradas nos.

IN the midst of life we are in death: what helper shall we seek save thee, O Lord, who art justly angry on account of our sins? O holy God, holy and strong, holy and merciful Redeemer, deliver us not to a bitter death.

V. Cast us not away in the time of our old age: when our strength shall fail, do not forsake us, O Lord.

O holy God, holy and strong, holy and merciful Redeemer, deliver us not to a bitter death.

III. *For the fifth and sixth weeks.*

O REX glorióse inter Sanctos tuos, qui semper es laudábilis et tamen ineffábilis: tu in nobis es, Dómine, et nomen sanctum tuum invocátum est super nos, ne derelínquas nos, Deus noster; ut in die judicii nos collocare dignéris inter sanctos et electos tuos, Rex benedicte.

O KING, glorious among thy saints, who art always adorable and still ineffable: thou art with us, O Lord, and thy name is invoked upon us; do not thou, our God, forsake us; that in the day of judgment thou mayst deign to place us among thy holy and chosen ones, O blessed King.

EASTER-DAY, AND THE WEEK FOLLOWING.

Only three Psalms are chanted, with the antiphon Alleluia, alleluia, alleluia, alleluia.
Then, the Chapter and Hymn being omitted, is sung immediately this Responsory:

H ÆC dies, quam fecit Dóminus : exultémus et lætémur in ea.

THIS is the day, which the Lord hath made : let us rejoice and be glad in it.

The Canticle Nunc dimittis *(page 19) follows, and after it this antiphon :*

Alleluia. Resurrexit Dóminus, alleluia : sicut dixit vobis, alleluia, alleluia.
V. Dóminus vobíscum.
R. Et cum spíritu tuo.

Alleluia. The Lord is risen, alleluia : as he said to you, alleluia, alleluia.
V. The Lord be with you.
R. And with thy spirit.

OREMUS.*

SPIRITUM nobis, Dómine, tuæ charitátis infúnde; ut quos Sacraméntis Paschálibus satiásti, tua facias pietáte concórdes. Per Dóminum nostrum Jesum Christum Fílium tuum, qui tecum vivit et regnat in unitáte ejúsdem, etc.
R. Amen.
V. Dominus vobiscum.
R. Et cum Spíritu tuo.
V. Benedicamus Domino.
R. Deo gratias.

LET US PRAY.

INFUSE into us, O Lord, the spirit of thy love, that of thy mercy thou mayst unite us in charity, whom thou hast satisfied with the Paschal Sacraments. Through our Lord Jesus Christ thy Son, who liveth and reigneth, etc.
R. Amen.
V. The Lord be with you.
R. And with thy spirit.
V. Let us bless the Lord.
R. Thanks be to God.

* On the Wednesday the usual prayer *Visita, quæsumus* (page 20) is resumed.

PASCHAL TIME.
From Low Sunday until the Eve of Trinity Sunday.

HYMN.

JESU nostra redémptio,
 Amor, et desidérium :
Deus creátor ómnium
Homo in fine témporum.

Quæ te vicit cleméntia,
Ut ferres nostra crímina,
Crudélem mortem pátiens,
Ut nos a morte tólleres.

Inferni claustra pénetrans,
Tuos captívos rédimens,
Victor triúmpho nóbili,
Ad dextram Patris residens.

Ipsa te cogat píetas,
Ut mala nostra súperes :
Parcéndo et voti cómpotes,
Nos tuo vultu sáties.

JESU, our ransom from
 above, [love,
Our sole desire, our sweetest
Creator God o'er all supreme,
Yet shrined within our
 fleshly frame.

What urgent mercy moved
 thy breast [that pressed
To bear the deadly weight
Our souls, and seek a death
 of pain, [reign ?
To free us from its ghastly

Piercing the shadowy depths
 of hell, [tives well,
Thou didst redeem thy cap-
Arising with thy triumph
 train, [to gain.
The Father's right-hand seat

Oh, let that mercy move
 thee still [every ill,
To fence us round from
And give our souls the
 crowning grace, [face.
To see the glories of thy

At Ascension and Whitsun-tide, see next pages.

Quaésumus auctor ómnium,
In hoc pascháli gaudio :
Ab omni mortis ímpetu,
Tuum defénde pópulum.

Glória tibi, Dómine,
Qui surrexísti a mórtuis,

We pray thee, maker of all
 things, [brings,
Amid the joy that Easter
From deadly sin's assaults
 defend [the end.
And shield thy people to

All glory, Lord, to thee we
 give, [to live
Who from the dead again

Cum Patre, et sancto Spíritu,
In sempitérna saécula.
Amen.

℣. Custódi nos Dómine ut pupíllum óculi. Allelúia.

℞. Sub umbra alárum tuárum prótege nos. Allelúia.

Didst rise, the everlasting Son,
With Father and with Spirit One. Amen.

℣. Keep us, O Lord, as the apple of thy eye. Alleluia.

℞. Protect us under the shadow of thy wings. Alleluia.

Nunc dimittis (*page* 19) *follows, and after it this antiphon*:

Allelúia. Resurréxit Dóminus, allelúia: sicut dixit vobis, allelúia, allelúia.

Alleluia. The Lord is risen, alleluia: as he said to you, alleluia, alleluia.

The rest as usual.

ASCENSION-DAY, AND DURING THE OCTAVE.

The last two verses of the Hymn are sung thus:

TU esto nostrum gáudium,
   Qui es futúrus praémium:
Sit nostra in te glória
Per cuncta semper saécula.

BE thou our present bliss,
   O Lord, [reward;
Who art our future great
And let our only glory be,
O Jesu, evermore in thee.

Glória tibi, Dómine,
Qui scandis supra sídera,
Cum Patre, et sancto Spíritu
In sempitérna saécula.
Amen.

All glory, Lord, to thee be given [to heaven,
Who soar'st above the stars
To reign, the everlasting Son,
With Father and with Spirit One. Amen.

Antiphon after Nunc dimittis.

Allelúia. Ascéndens Christus in altum, allelúia: captívam duxit captivitátem, allelúia, allelúia.

Alleluia. Christ ascending on high, alleluia: led captivity captive, alleluia, alleluia.

WHITSUN-DAY, AND WEEK FOLLOWING.

The last two verses of the Hymn are sung thus:

DUDUM sacráta péctora
   Tua replésti grátia:
Dimítte nunc peccámina
Et da quiéta témpora.

LONG since thy grace thou
   didst impart, [heart:
To dwell in each disciple's
With the same grace our
   sins release, [give peace.
And in our times, O Lord,

Sit laus Patri cum Fílio
Sancto simul Paráclito:
Nobísque mittat Fílius
Charísma sancti Spíritus.
    Amen.

To Sire and Son be praises
   meet,
And to the holy Paraclete;
And may Christ send us
   from above
That Holy Spirit's gift of
   love. Amen.

Antiphon after Nunc dimittis.

Allelúia. Spíritus paráclitus, allelúia: docébit vos ómnia, allelúia, allelúia.

Alleluia. The Spirit, the Paraclete, alleluia: will teach you all things, alleluia, alleluia.

CORPUS CHRISTI, AND DURING THE OCTAVE.

The third verse of the Hymn Te lucis ante terminum *is sung thus:*

GLORIA tibi, Dómine,
   Qui natus es de Vírgine,
Cum Patre et sancto Spíritu,
In sempitérna sæcula.
    Amen.

ALL glory be to thee, O
   Lord, [adored,
A Virgin's Son, o'er all
And equal praise for ever
   greet,
The Father and the Paraclete. Amen.

Antiphon after Nunc dimittis.

Alleluia. Panis quem ego dédero, allelúia: caro mea est pro mundi vita, allelúia, allelúia.

Alleluia. The Bread which I will give, alleluia: is my Flesh for the life of the world, alleluia, alleluia.

FEASTS OF THE BLESSED VIRGIN,
AND THE
OCTAVES OF HER IMMACULATE CONCEPTION AND ASSUMPTION.

ANTIPHONS.

I. *After the Psalms.*

VIRGO María, non est tibi símilis nata in mundo inter mulíeres ; florens ut rosa fragrans sicut lílium : ora pro nobis, sancta Dei Génitrix.

O VIRGIN Mary, there is none born in this world amongst women like unto thee ; blooming as a rose, fragrant as a lily : pray for us, O holy Mother of God.

II. *After* Nunc dimittis.

CORDE et ánimo Christo canámus glóriam in hac sacra solemnitáte præcélsæ Genitrícis Dei Maríæ.

WITH heart and soul let us sing glory to Christ on this sacred solemnity of Mary the illustrious Mother of God.

III. *After* Nunc dimittis *on the Assumption and certain other Feasts.*

SUB tuum præsídium confúgimus, sancta Dei Génitrix : nostras deprecatiónes ne despícias in necessitátibus, sed a perículis cunctis líbera nos semper Virgo benedícta.

WE fly to thy patronage, O holy mother of God ; despise not our prayers in our necessities, but deliver us from all dangers, O everglorious and blessed Virgin.

PURIFICATION.

IV. *After the Psalms.*

SANCTA Dei Génitrix, Virgo semper Maria, intercéde pro nobis ad Dóminum Deum nostrum.

HOLY Mother of God, Mary ever Virgin, intercede for us unto the Lord our God.

V. *After* Nunc dimittis.

NUNC dimíttis, Dómine, servum tuum in pace, quia vidérunt óculi mei salutáre tuum.

NOW dost thou dismiss thy servant, O Lord, in peace ; for mine eyes have seen thy salvation.

COMPLINE.

ANNUNCIATION, AND DURING THE OCTAVE.

VI. *After the Psalms.*

ECCE Virgo concípiet, et páriet Fílium; et vocábitur nomen ejus Emmánuel.

BEHOLD a Virgin shall conceive, and bear a Son: and his name shall be called Emmanuel.

VII. *After* Nunc dimittis.

ECCE ancílla Dómini: fiat mihi secúndum verbum tuum.

BEHOLD the handmaid of the Lord: be it done unto me according to thy word.

At the Hymn, in place of Præsta, Pater omnipotens, *the following verses are sung:*

MARIA, mater grátiæ,
  Mater misericórdiæ,
Tu nos ab hoste prótege,
Et hora mortis súscipe.

O MARY, mother of all
  grace   [race,
And mercy to our sinful
Protect us from the demon's
  power,   [hour.
And take us at life's closing

Glória tibi, Dómine,
Qui natus es de Vírgine,
Cum Patre et sancto Spíritu,
In sempitérna sæcula.
                Amen.

All glory be to thee, O Lord,
A Virgin's Son, o'er all
  adored,   [greet
And equal praise for ever
The Father and the Paraclete. Amen.

HYMNS.

Advent.

En clara vox redarguit.

HARK, an awful voice is sounding;
   'Christ is nigh,' it seems to say;
'Cast away the dreams of darkness,
   O ye children of the day!'

Startled at the solemn warning,
   Let the earth-bound soul arise;
Christ her Sun, all sloth dispelling,
   Shines upon the morning skies.

Lo, the Lamb so long expected
   Comes with pardon down from heaven;
Let us haste with tears of sorrow,
   One and all to be forgiven.

So when next he comes with glory,
   Wrapping all the earth in fear,
May he then, as our defender,
   On the clouds of heaven appear.

Honour, glory, virtue, merit,
   To the Father and the Son,
With the co-eternal Spirit,
   While eternal ages run.

Advent.

Creator alme siderum.

DEAR Maker of the starry skies,
    Light of believers evermore,
Jesu, Redeemer of mankind,
    Be near us who thine aid implore.

When man was sunk in sin and death,
    Lost in the depth of Satan's snare,
Love brought thee down to cure our ills,
    By taking of those ills a share.

Thou, for the sake of guilty men,
    Permitting thy pure blood to flow,
Didst issue from thy Virgin shrine,
    And to the cross a Victim go.

So great the glory of thy might,
    If we but chance thy name to sound,
At once all heaven and hell unite
    In bending low with awe profound.

Great Judge of all, in that last day,
    When friends shall fail, and foes combine,
Be present then with us, we pray,
    To guard us with thy arm divine.

To God the Father, with the Son,
    And Holy Spirit, One and Three,
Be honour, glory, blessing, praise,
    All through the long eternity.

Advent.

Our Lady's Expectation.

LIKE the dawning of the morning,
  On the mountains' golden heights,
Like the breaking of the moonbeams
  On the gloom of cloudy nights,
Like a secret told by angels,
  Getting known upon the earth,
Is the Mother's expectation
  Of Messiah's speedy birth.

Thou wert happy, blessed Mother,
  With the very bliss of heaven,
Since the angel's salutation
  In thy raptured ear was given;
Since the Ave of that midnight
  When thou wert anointed Queen,
Like a river overflowing
  Hath the grace within thee been.

Thou hast waited, child of David,
  And thy waiting now is o'er;
Thou hast seen him, blessed Mother,
  And wilt see him evermore.
Oh, his human face and features,
  They were passing sweet to see;
Thou beholdest them this moment;
  Mother, show them now to me.

Christmas.

Gloria in excelsis Deo.

ANGELS we have heard on high,
    Sweetly singing o'er our plains,
And the mountains in reply
    Echoing their joyous strains.
        Gloria in excelsis Deo.

Shepherds, why this jubilee?
    Why your rapturous strain prolong?
What the gladsome tidings be
    Which inspire your heavenly song?
        Gloria in excelsis Deo.

Come to Bethlehem, and see
    Him whose birth the angels sing;
Come, adore on bended knee
    Christ the Lord, the new-born King.
        Gloria in excelsis Deo.

See him in a manger laid,
    Whom the choirs of angels praise.
Mary, Joseph, lend your aid,
    While our hearts in love we raise.
        Gloria in excelsis Deo.

Christmas.

Adeste, fideles.

ADESTE, fidéles,
   Læti triumphántes;
Veníte, veníte in Béthlehem;
  Natum vidéte
  Regem angelórum:
  Veníte adorémus,
  Veníte adorémus,
Veníte adorémus Dóminum.

  Deum de Deo,
  Lumen de lúmine,
Gestant puéllæ víscera;
  Deum verum,
  Génitum, non factum:
  Veníte adorémus,
  Veníte adorémus,
Veníte adorémus Dóminum.

  Cantet nunc Io
  Chorus angelórum,
Cantet nunc aula cœléstium,
  Glória
  In excélsis Deo;
  Veníte adorémus,
  Veníte adorémus,
Veníte adorémus Dóminum.

  Ergo qui natus
  Die hodiérna,
Jesu tibi sit glória;
  Patris ætérni
  Verbum caro factum:
  Veníte adorémus,
  Veníte adorémus,
Veníte adorémus Dóminum.

Christmas.

Adeste, fideles.

YE faithful, approach ye,
    Joyfully triumphing;
Oh come ye, oh come ye, to Bethlehem:
Come and behold him
Born the King of angels:
    Oh come, let us adore him,
    Oh come, let us adore him,
Oh come, let us adore him, Christ the Lord.

God of God,
Light of Light,
Lo, he disdains not the Virgin's womb;
Very God,
Begotten, not created:
    Oh come, let us adore him,
    Oh come, let us adore him.
Oh come, let us adore him, Christ the Lord.

Sing Alleluia
All ye choirs of angels,
Sing, all ye citizens of heaven above,
Glory to God
In the highest:
    Oh come, let us adore him,
    Oh come, let us adore him,
Oh come, let us adore him, Christ the Lord.

Yea, Lord, we greet thee,
Born this happy morning;
Jesu, to thee be glory given:
Word of the Father
Now in flesh appearing:
    Oh come, let us adore him,
    Oh come, let us adore him,
Oh come, let us adore him, Christ the Lord.

Christmas.

Hail, thou ever-blessed morn.

SEE, amid the winter's snow,
   Born for us on earth below ;
See, the tender Lamb appears,
Promised from eternal years !
     Hail, thou ever-blessed morn,
     Hail, Redemption's happy dawn !
     Sing through all Jerusalem,
     Christ is born in Bethlehem !

Lo, within a manger lies
He who built the starry skies ;
He, who throned in height sublime,
Sits amid the Cherubim !
     Hail, thou ever-blessed morn, etc.

Sacred Infant all divine,
What a tender love was thine ;
Thus to come from highest bliss,
Down to such a world as this !
     Hail, thou ever-blessed morn, etc.

Teach, oh teach us, holy Child,
By thy face so meek and mild ;
Teach us to resemble thee
In thy sweet humility.
     Hail, thou ever-blessed morn, etc.

Virgin Mother, Mary blest,
By the joys that fill thy breast,
Pray for us that we may prove
Worthy of the Saviour's love.
     Hail, thou ever-blessed morn,
     Hail, Redemption's happy dawn !
     Sing through all Jerusalem,
     Christ is born in Bethlehem !

Christmas.

Shepherds at the Manger.

STARS of glory, shine more brightly,
   Purer be the moonlight's beam,
Glide ye hours and moments lightly,
   Swiftly down time's deepening stream :
Bring the hour that banished sadness,
   Brought redemption down to earth,
When the shepherds heard with gladness
   Tidings of a Saviour's birth.

See a beauteous angel soaring
   In the bright celestial blaze,
On the shepherds low adoring
   Rest his mild, effulgent rays :
'Fear not'—cries the heavenly stranger—
   'Him whom ancient seers foretold,
Weeping in a lowly manger,
   Shepherds, haste ye to behold.'

See the shepherds quickly rising,
   Hastening to the humble stall,
And the new-born Infant prizing,
   As the mighty Lord of all ;
Lowly now they bend before him,
   In his helpless infant state,
Firmly faithful they adore him
   And his greatness celebrate.

Hark the swell of heavenly voices
   Peals along the vaulted sky ;
Angels sing, while earth rejoices—
   'Glory to our God on high ;
Glory in the highest heaven,
   Peace to humble men on earth ;
Joy to these and bliss is given,
   In the great Redeemer's birth.'

Epiphany.

Quæ stella sole pulchrior.

WHAT beauteous sun-surpassing star
   O'er Bethlehem's lonely road,
Reveals a rising brighter far,
   And shows the cradled God.
The star from Jacob see arise,
   By prophets long foretold;
Ye Eastern nations, in the skies
   His messenger behold.

While thus the star its light imparts,
   A ray within doth shine,
Which leads a few but faithful hearts
   To seek the glorious sign.
No dangers can their purpose shake;
   Love suffers no delay;
Home, kindred, country, they forsake;
   God calls, and they obey.

Jesu, bright morning Star, our hearts
   Cleanse with thy light within;
And suffer not the tempter's arts
   To lure us back to sin.
The Light of Gentile lands adore,
   The Day-spring from on high,
Alike the Father evermore,
   And Spirit magnify.

Holy Name of Jesus.

10

Jesu, dulcis memoria.

JESUS, the only thought of thee
  With sweetness fills my breast;
But sweeter far it is to see,
  And on thy beauty feast.

No sound, no harmony so gay,
  Can art of music frame;
No words, nor even thought can say,
  The sweets of thy blest name.

Jesus, our hope, when we repent,
  Sweet source of all our grace;
Sole comfort in our banishment,
  Oh what when face to face!

Jesus, that name inspires my mind,
  With springs of life and light;
More than I ask in thee I find,
  And languish with delight.

No art or eloquence of man
  Can tell the joys of love;
Only the saints can understand
  What they in Jesus prove.

Jesu, our only joy be thou,
  As thou our prize wilt be;
Jesu, be thou our glory now
  And through eternity.

Also 71, 72.

Lent.

11

Audi, benigne Conditor.

O GRACIOUS Lord, Creator dear,
  In mercy lend a pitying ear
Unto the mournful prayer we pour
In this our solemn Lenten hour.

Thou who our secret thoughts canst trace
And knowst the frailty of our race—
Like wandering sheep we went astray—
Oh, take us back, we meekly pray.

Black is our guilt and great our shame;
But for the glory of thy name,
Forgive the wickedness we own,
And heal the wounds for which we groan.

Grant us by holy abstinence
To mortify each carnal sense;
That so our souls, from sin set free,
May rise all-holy unto thee.

Blest Three in One, with grief sincere,
Before thy footstool we appear;
Oh, bless our fast, that it may prove
The source of pardon, peace, and love.

Lent.

Solemne nos jejunii.

AGAIN the time appointed see,
   That calls to fast and sigh
Let priest and people bend the knee,
   And loud for mercy cry.

But vain all outward form of grief,
   And vain the word of prayer,
Unless the heart desire relief,
   And penitence be there.

The forehead prostrate in the dust,
   The hair and garments torn,
Can never stay the vengeance just,
   Unless the conscience mourn.

Then, let us to the Lord draw near
   With tears that contrite flow ;
By reverence and godly fear
   We may escape the woe.

O holy judge, O Christ, relent,
   Thine arm uplifted stay ;
And grant a season to repent,
   A time in which to pray.

Great Three in One, thy name we bless,
   Thy praises ever sing ;
Oh, grant that fruits of righteousness
   From Lenten tears may spring.

Lent.

13

Oh, hearken when we cry.

NOW are the days of humblest prayer,
  When consciences to God lie bare,
And mercy most delights to spare.
Oh, hearken when we cry; chastise us with thy fear;
Yet, Father, in the multitude of thy compassions, hear.

Now is the season, wisely long,
Of sadder thought and graver song,
When ailing souls grow well and strong.
Oh, hearken when we cry; chastise us with thy fear;
Yet, Father, in the multitude of thy compassions, hear.

The feast of penance—oh, so bright,
With true conversion's heavenly light,
Like sunrise after stormy night.
Oh, hearken when we cry; chastise us with thy fear;
Yet, Father, in the multitude of thy compassions, hear.

O happy time of blessed tears,
Of surer hopes, of chastening fears,
Undoing all our evil years.
Oh, hearken when we cry; chastise us with thy fear;
Yet, Father, in the multitude of thy compassions, hear.

We, who have loved the world, must learn
Upon that world our backs to turn,
And with the love of God to burn.
Oh, hearken when we cry; chastise us with thy fear;
Yet, Father, in the multitude of thy compassions, hear.

Also **65, 66, 67.**

Lent.

Psalm 50.

MISERERE mei, Deus : * secúndum magnam misericórdiam tuam.

2. Et secúndum multitúdinem miseratiónum túarum : * dele iniquitátem meam.

3. Amplius lava me ab iniquitáte mea : * et a peccáto meo munda me.

4. Quóniam iniquitátem meam ego cognósco : * et peccátum meum contra me est semper.

5. Tibi soli peccávi, et malum coram te feci : * ut justificéris in sermónibus tuis, et vincas cum judicáris.

6. Ecce enim in iniquitátibus concéptus sum : * et in peccátis concépit me mater mea.

7. Ecce enim veritátem dilexísti : * incérta et occúlta sapiéntiæ tuæ manifestásti mihi.

8. Aspérges me hyssópo, et mundábor : * lavábis me, et super nivem dealbábor.

9. Audítui meo dabis gaúdium et lætítiam : * et exultábunt ossa humiliáta.

10. Avérte faciem tuam a

HAVE mercy upon me, O God : according to thy great mercy.

And according to the multitude of thy tender mercies : blot out my iniquity.

Wash me yet more from my iniquity : and cleanse me from my sin.

For I acknowledge my iniquity : and my sin is always before me.

Against thee only have I sinned, and done evil in thy sight : that thou mayest be justified in thy words, and mayest overcome when thou art judged.

For behold, I was conceived in iniquities : and in sins did my mother conceive me.

For behold, thou hast loved truth : the uncertain and hidden things of thy wisdom thou hast made manifest unto me.

Thou shalt sprinkle me with hyssop, and I shall be cleansed : thou shalt wash me, and I shall be made whiter than snow.

Thou shalt make me hear of joy and gladness : and the bones that were humbled shall rejoice.

Turn away thy face from

peccátis meis : * et omnes iniquitátes meas dele.

11. Cor mundum crea in me, Deus : * et spíritum rectum ínnova in viscéribus meis.

12. Ne projícias me a fácie tua : * et Spíritum sanctum tuum ne áuferas a me.

13. Redde mihi lætítiam salutáris tui : * et spíritu principali confírma me.

14. Docébo iníquos vias tuas : * et impii ad te converténtur.

15. Líbera me de sanguínibus, Deus, Deus salútis meæ : * et exultábit lingua mea justítiam tuam.

16. Dómine, lábia mea apéries : * et os meum annuntiábit laudem tuam.

17. Quóniam si voluísses sacrifícium, dedíssem utique : * holocáustis non delectáberis.

18. Sacrifícium Deo spiritus contribulátus : * cor contrítum et humiliátum, Deus, non despícies.

19. Benígne fac, Dómine, in bona voluntáte tua Sion : * ut ædificéntur muri Jerúsalem.

20. Tunc acceptábis sacrifícium justítiæ, oblatiónes, et holocáusta : * tunc impónent super altáre tuum vítulos.

Glória Patri, etc.

my sins : and blot out all my iniquities.

Create in me a clean heart, O God : and renew a right spirit within my bowels.

Cast me not away from thy presence : and take not thy holy Spirit from me.

Restore unto me the joy of thy salvation : and strengthen me with a perfect spirit.

I will teach the unjust thy ways : and the wicked shall be converted unto thee.

Deliver me from blood-guiltiness, O God, thou God of my salvation : and my tongue shall extol thy justice.

Thou shalt open my lips, O Lord : and my mouth shall declare thy praise.

For if thou hadst desired sacrifice, I would surely have given it : with burnt offerings thou wilt not be delighted.

The sacrifice of God is an afflicted spirit : a contrite and humble heart, O God, thou wilt not despise.

Deal favourably, O Lord, in thy good will, with Sion : that the walls of Jerusalem may be built up.

Then shalt thou accept the sacrifice of justice, oblations, and whole burnt offerings : then shall they lay calves upon thine altars.

Glory be to the Father, etc.

Passion-Tide.

Stabat Mater dolorosa.

STABAT Mater dolorósa,
  Juxta crucem lacrymósa,
    Dum pendébat Fílius.

Cujus ánimam geméntem,
Contristátam, et doléntem,
    Pertransívit gládius.

O quam tristis et afflicta
Fuit illa benedícta
    Mater Unigéniti!

Quæ mœrébat, et dolébat,
Pia Mater dum vidébat
    Nati pœnas ínclyti.

Quis est homo, qui non fleret,
Matrem Christi si vidéret
    In tanto supplício?

Quis non posset contristári,
Christi Matrem contemplári
    Doléntem cum Fílio?

Pro peccátis suæ géntis,
Vidit Jesum in torméntis,
    Et flagéllis súbditum.

Vidit suum dulcem natum
Moriéndo, desolátum,
    Dum emísit spíritum.

Eia Mater, fons amóris,
Me sentíre vim dolóris
    Fac, ut tecum lúgeam.

Fac ut árdeat cor meum
In amándo Christum Deum,
    Ut sibi compláceam.

WEEPING sore, the Mother
  stood
Nigh the cross, the fatal wood,
Whereon hung her dying Son.

Through her soul for anguish
  crying,   (sighing,
Sunk in sorrow, spent with
The prophetic sword had run.

Oh, how sad, how heavy laden,
Was that meek and blessed
  Maiden,
God's true Mother undefiled:

Trembling, grieving, whelmed
  in woes,
When she saw the dying throes
Of her own immortal Child:

Who is he whose weeping eyes
Would not choose but sym-
  pathise
With the Mother of our Lord?

Who is he that would refuse
Pity for such Mother's woes,
Weeping o'er her Son adored?

Tortured for his sinful race,
She beheld each ghastly trace
Of his scourging at the post.

She beheld her Son so sweet
Dying and all desolate
When he yielded up the ghost.

Come, dear Mother, love's sweet
  spring,
Let me share thy sorrowing,
Let my tears unite with thine.

Let my heart be wrapt in fire
Still to seek with fond desire
  Christ my God, my love
    divine.

PASSION-TIDE.

Sancta Mater, istud agas,
Crucifixi fige plagas
　Cordi meo válide.

Tui Nati vulneráti,
Tam dignáti pro me pati,
　Poenas mecum divide.

Fac me tecum pie flere,
Crucifixo condoléré,
　Donec ego víxero.

Juxta crucem tecum stare,
Et me tibi sociáre,
　In planctu desídero.

Virgo vírginum præclára,
Mihi jam non sis amára
　Fac me tecum plángere.

Fac ut portem Christi mortem,
Passiónis fac consórtem,
　Et plagas recólere.

Fac me plagis vulnerári,
Fac me cruce inebriári,
　Et cruóre Filii.

Flammis ne urar succénsus
Per te, Virgo, sim defensus
　In die judícii.

Christe, cum sit hinc exíre,
Da per Matrem me veníre
　Ad palmam victóriæ.

Quando corpus moriétur,
Fac ut ánimæ donétur
　Paradísi glória. Amen.

Holy Mother, this impart,
Deeply print upon my heart
　All the wounds he dying bore.

Let me share his pains with thee,
Who so tenderly for me
　Deigned those sorrows to endure.

Let our tears in one same tide
Flow for Jesus crucified,
　Long as life shall warm my breast.

By the cross to take my station,
Share thy tender lamentation,
　This is my most fond request.

Brightest of the virgin-train,
Do not thou my suit disdain,
　Come and share thy grief with me.

Let me trace his sufferings o'er,
Bear the very death he bore,
　When they nailed him to the tree:

Feel the wounds he felt for us,
Drink the chalice of his cross,
　All for love of thy dear Son.

Screened by thee from flames divine,
Mary, guard this soul of mine
　When the judgment-day comes on.

Christ, when these my days are done,
Let thy Mother lead me on
　To the palm of victory:

Yea, when this frail flesh hath died,
Let my soul be glorified
　Safe in paradise with thee.
　Amen.

This hymn is commonly used during the devotion of the *Way of the Cross*, a verse being sung as the procession moves between the Stations.

Passion-Tide.

16

Sævo dolorum turbine.

O'ERWHELMED in depths of woe,
  Upon the tree of scorn
Hangs the Redeemer of mankind,
  With racking anguish torn.

See, how the nails those hands
  And feet so tender rend;
See, down his face and neck and breast
  His sacred blood descend.

Hark, with what awful cry
  His Spirit takes its flight;
That cry, it smote his Mother's heart,
  And wrapt her soul in night.

Earth hears, and to its base
  Rocks wildly to and fro;
Tombs burst; seas, rivers—mountains quake;
  The veil is rent in two.

The sun withdraws his light;
  The midday heavens grow pale;
The moon, the stars, the universe,
  Their maker's death bewail.

Shall man alone be mute?
  Come, youth and hoary hairs;
Come, rich and poor; come, all mankind,
  And bathe those feet in tears.

Come, fall before his cross,
  Who shed for us his blood;
Who died the victim of pure love,
  To make us sons of God.

Jesu, all praise to thee,
  Our joy and endless rest:
Be thou our guide while pilgrims here,
  Our crown amid the blest.

Passion-Tide.

17

Jesus, our Love, is crucified.

OH, come and mourn with me awhile;
  See, Mary calls us to her side;
Oh, come and let us mourn with her:
  Jesus, our Love, is crucified.

Have we no tears to shed for him,
While soldiers scoff and Jews deride?
Ah, look how patiently he hangs:
  Jesus, our Love, is crucified.

What was thy crime, my dearest Lord?
By earth, by heaven, thou hast been tried,
And guilty found of too much love:
  Jesus, our Love, is crucified.

Oh break, oh break, hard heart of mine,
Thy weak self-love and guilty pride
His Pilate and his Judas were:
  Jesus, our Love, is crucified.

Come take thy stand beneath the cross,
And let the blood from out that side
Fall gently on thee drop by drop:
  Jesus, our Love, is crucified.

O love of God, O sin of man,
In this dread act your strength is tried;
And victory remains with love—
  For he, our Love, is crucified.

Passion-Tide.

Meditation on the Passion.

MY Jesus, say, what wretch has dared
    Thy sacred hands to bind ?
And who has dared to buffet so
    Thy face so meek and kind ?
      'Tis I have thus ungrateful been,
        Yet, Jesus, pity take ;
      Oh, spare and pardon me, my Lord,
        For thy sweet mercy's sake.

My Jesus, who with spittle vile
    Profaned thy sacred brow ?
And whose unpitying scourge has made
    Thy precious blood to flow ?
      'Tis I have thus ungrateful been, etc.

My Jesus, whose the hands that wove
    That cruel thorny crown ?
Who made that hard and heavy cross
    Which weighs thy shoulders down ?
      'Tis I have thus ungrateful been, etc.

My Jesus, who has mocked thy thirst
    With vinegar and gall ?
Who held the nails that pierced thy hands,
    And made the hammer fall ?
      'Tis I have thus ungrateful been, etc.

My Jesus, say who dared to nail
    Those tender feet of thine ?
And whose the arm that raised the lance
    To pierce that heart divine ?
      'Tis I have thus ungrateful been, etc.

And Mary, who has murdered thus
    Thy loved and only One ?
Canst thou forgive the blood-stained hand
    That robbed thee of thy Son ?
      'Tis I have thus ungrateful been,
        To Jesus and to thee ;
      Forgive me for thy Jesus' sake,
        And pray to him for me.

Passion-Tide.

19

Mary sorrowing.

WHAT a sea of tears and sorrow
    Did the soul of Mary toss
To and fro upon its billows,
    While she wept her bitter loss;
In her arms her Jesus holding,
    Torn so newly from the cross.

Oh that mournful Virgin-Mother,
    See her tears how fast they flow
Down upon his mangled body,
    Wounded side, and thorny brow;
While his hands and feet she kisses,—
    Picture of immortal woe.

Oft and oft his arms and bosom
    Fondly straining to her own;
Oft her pallid lips imprinting
    On each wound of her dear Son;
Till at last, in swoons of anguish,
    Sense and consciousness are gone.

Gentle Mother, we beseech thee,
    By thy tears and troubles sore;
By the death of thy dear Offspring,
    By the bloody wounds he bore;
Touch our hearts with that true sorrow
    Which afflicted thee of yore.

Also **34, 70.**

Easter.

Aurora cœlum purpurat.

THE dawn was purpling o'er the sky ;
  With alleluias rang the air ;
Earth held a glorious jubilee ;
  Hell gnashed its teeth in fierce despair :

When our most valiant mighty king
  From death's abyss, in dread array,
Led the long-prisoned Fathers forth,
  Into the beam of life and day :

When he, whom stone and seal and guard
  Had safely to the tomb consigned,
Triumphant rose, and buried death
  Deep in the grave he left behind.

'Calm all your grief, and still your tears,'
  Hark, the descending angel cries ;
'For Christ is risen from the dead,
  And death is slain, no more to rise.'

O Jesu, from the death of sin
  Keep us, we pray ; so shalt thou be
The everlasting paschal joy
  Of all the souls new-born in thee.

To God the Father, with the Son
  Who from the grave immortal rose,
And thee, O Paraclete, be praise
  While age on endless ages flows.

Easter.

O filii et filiæ.

ALLELUIA.   ALLELUIA.   ALLELUIA.

YE sons and daughters of the Lord,
   The king of glory, king adored,
This day himself from death restored.
                            Alleluia.

All in the early morning grey
Went holy women on their way,
To see the tomb where Jesus lay.   Alleluia.

Then straightway one in white they see,
Who saith, 'Ye seek the Lord; but he
Is risen, and gone to Galilee.'   Alleluia.

That self-same night, while out of fear
The doors were shut, their Lord most dear
To his apostles did appear.   Alleluia.

But Thomas, when of this he heard,
Was doubtful of his brethren's word;
Wherefore again there comes the Lord.
                            Alleluia.

'Thomas, behold my side,' saith he;
'My hands, my feet, my body see,
And doubt not, but believe in me.'   Alleluia.

When Thomas saw that wounded side,
The truth no longer he denied;
'Thou art my Lord and God,' he cried.
                            Alleluia.

Oh, blest are they who have not seen
Their Lord, and yet believe in him:
Eternal life awaiteth them.   Alleluia.

Now let us praise the Lord most high,
And strive his name to magnify
On this great day, through earth and sky.
                            Alleluia.

Easter.

Jesus risen.

ALL hail, dear Conqueror, all hail;
  Oh, what a victory is thine,
How beautiful thy strength appears,
  Thy crimson wounds how bright they shine.

Thou camest at the dawn of day;
  Armies of souls around thee were,
Blest spirits thronging to adore
  Thy flesh, so marvellous, so fair.

The everlasting Godhead lay
  Shrouded within those limbs divine,
Nor left untenanted one hour
  That sacred human heart of thine.

They worshipped thee, those ransomed souls,
  With the fresh strength of love set free;
They worshipped joyously, and thought;
  Of Mary while they looked on thee.

They worshipped, while the beauteous Soul
  Paused by the Body's wounded side:
Bright flashed the cave—before them stood
  The living Jesus glorified.

Down, down, all lofty things on earth,
  And worship him with joyous dread;
O sin, thou art undone by love;
  O death, thou art discomfited.

Ascension.

Opus peregisti tuum.

THY sacred race, O Lord, is run,
   Thy work is wrought, thy victory won ;
The glory thou didst leave requires
Thy presence in supernal choirs.
The clouds thy chariot, earth afar
Beneath thy feet, a little star ;
Ten thousand thousand angels sing,
To welcome their returning king.

   The gates of heaven obey the call,
And open to the Lord of all ;
His throne receives the eternal Son,
Both God and Man for ever one.
Thou Mediator and high-priest,
Fresh from the sacrifice released,
By love constrained dost hither bring
Thy smitten heart's best offering.

   And she who from thy opened side
Her being took, thy holy Bride,
Still nourished from thy side survives,
And life and all from thee derives.
Hence, in the thickest of the fight,
Thy warriors win their heavenly might ;
And hence, thy martyrs sing their psalms,
And joyous wave triumphal palms.

   Where thou, the head, art gone, thy voice
Calls all thy members to rejoice ;
Ah, let them cleave the shining way,
Thy footprints through the ether fray.
To thee be glory, conquering king,
Who unto heaven thy way dost wing,
Great Son of the eternal Sire,
Whose Spirit is our one desire.

Whitsun-Tide.

24

Veni, sancte Spiritus.

HOLY Spirit, come and shine
On our souls with beams divine,
  Issuing from thy radiance bright.

Come, O Father of the poor,
Ever bounteous of thy store,
  Come, our hearts' unfailing light.

Come, consoler, kindest, best,
Come, our bosom's dearest guest,
  Sweet refreshment, sweet repose.

Rest in labour, coolness sweet,
Tempering the burning heat,
  Truest comfort of our woes.

O divinest light, impart
Unto every faithful heart
  Plenteous streams from love's bright flood.

But for thy blest Deity,
Nothing pure in man could be;
  Nothing harmless, nothing good.

Wash away each sinful stain;
Gently shed thy gracious rain
  On the dry and fruitless soul.

Heal each wound and bend each will,
Warm our hearts benumbed and chill,
  All our wayward steps control.

Unto all thy faithful just,
Who in thee confide and trust,
  Deign the seven-fold gift to send.

Grant us virtue's blest increase,
Grant a death of hope and peace,
  Grant the joys that never end.

Whitsun-Tide.

Veni, Creator Spiritus.

VENI, Creátor Spíritus,
    Mentes tuórum vísita,
Imple supérna grátia
Quæ tu creásti péctora.

Qui Paraclétus díceris
Donum Dei Altíssimi,
Fons vivus, ignis, cháritas,
Et spiritális unetio.

Tu septifórmis munere,
Dextræ Dei tu dígitus,
Tu rite promíssum Patris,
Sermóne ditans gúttura.

Accénde lumen sénsibus,
Infúnde amórem córdibus,
Infírma nostri córporis
Virtúte fírmans pérpeti.

Hostem repéllas lóngius,
Pacémque dones prótinus:
Ductóre sic te praévio,
Vitémus omne nóxium.

Per te sciámus da Patrem,
Noscámus atque Filium,
Te utriúsque Spíritum
Credámus omni témpore.

Sit laus Patri cum Fílio,
Sancto simul Paráclito:
Nobísque mittat Fílius
Charísma sancti Spíritus.
               Amen.

Whitsun-Tide.

Veni, Creator Spiritus.

CREATOR-SPIRIT, all-divine,
  Come visit every soul of thine,
And fill with thy celestial flame
The hearts which thou thyself didst frame.

O gift of God, thine is the sweet
Consoling name of Paraclete—
And spring of life and fire and love
And unction flowing from above.

The mystic seven-fold gifts are thine,
Finger of God's right hand divine;
The Father's promise sent to teach
The tongue a rich and heavenly speech.

Kindle with fire brought from above
Each sense, and fill our hearts with love;
And grant our flesh, so weak and frail,
The strength of thine which ne'er may fail.

Drive far away our deadly foe,
And grant us thy true peace to know;
So we, led by thy guidance still,
Safely may pass through every ill.

To us, through thee, the grace be shown
To know the Father and the Son;
And Spirit of them both, may we
For ever rest our faith in thee.

To Sire and Son be praises meet,
And to the holy Paraclete;
And may Christ send us from above
That Holy Spirit's gift of love.
                    Amen.

Whitsun-Tide.

27

To the Holy Ghost.

HOLY Ghost, come down upon thy children,
  Give us grace and make us thine;
Thy tender fires within us kindle,
  Blessed Spirit, Dove divine.

For all within us good and holy
  Is from thee, thy precious gift;
In all our joys, in all our sorrows,
  Wistful hearts to thee we lift.
    Holy Ghost, etc.

For thou to us art more than father,
  More than sister, in thy love,
So gentle, patient, and forbearing,
  Holy Spirit, heavenly Dove.
    Holy Ghost, etc.

Oh, we have grieved thee, gracious Spirit,
  Wayward, wanton, cold are we;
And still our sins, new every morning,
  Never yet have wearied thee.
    Holy Ghost, etc.

Dear Paraclete, how hast thou waited
  While our hearts were slowly turned;
How often hath thy love been slighted,
  While for us it grieved and burned.
    Holy Ghost, etc.

Now, if our hearts do not deceive us,
  We would take thee for our Lord;
O dearest Spirit, make us faithful
  To thy least and lightest word.
    Holy Ghost, come down upon thy children,
      Give us grace and make us thine;
    Thy tender fires within us kindle,
      Blessed Spirit, Dove divine.

Trinity Sunday.

The Most Holy Trinity.

HAVE mercy on us, God most high,
   Who lift our hearts to thee ;
Have mercy on us worms of earth,
   Most holy Trinity.

When heaven and earth were yet unmade,
   When time was yet unknown,
Thou in thy bliss and majesty
   Didst live and love alone.

How wonderful creation is,
   The work that thou didst bless ;
And oh, what then must thou be like,
   Eternal loveliness.

O majesty most beautiful,
   Most holy Trinity,
On Mary's throne we climb to get
   A far-off sight of thee.

Oh listen, then, most pitiful,
   To thy poor creature's heart ;
It blesses thee that thou art God,
   That thou art what thou art.

Most ancient of all mysteries,
   Before thy throne we lie ;
Have mercy now, most merciful,
   Most holy Trinity.

Also **68**.

Corpus Christi.

29

AT THE PROCESSION.

Pange lingua gloriosi corporis.

PANGE lingua gloriósi
　Córporis mystérium,
Sanguinísque pretiósi,
　Quem in mundi pretium
Fructus ventris generósi
　Rex effúdit géntium.

Nobis datus, nobis natus
　Ex intácta Vírgine ;
Et in mundo conversátus,
　Sparso verbi sémine,
Sui moras incolátus
　Miro clausit órdine.

In suprémæ nocte cœnæ
　Recúmbens cum frátribus,
Observáta lege plene
　Cibis in legálibus,
Cibum turbæ duodénæ
　Se dat suis mánibus.

Verbum caro, panem verum
　Verbo, carnem éfficit,
Fitque sanguis Christi merum ;
　Et si sensus déficit,
Ad firmándum cor sincérum
　Sola fides súfficit.

SING, my joyful tongue, the
　mystery
Of the glorious body slain,
And the blood all pure and
　precious
Shed a lost world to regain,
By the king of nations, issuing
From a womb that knew no
　stain.

Born unto us of a Virgin
　Purer than the purest snow,
And amongst mankind con-
　versing　　　　　　[sow,
Seeds of heavenly truth to
He at length in wondrous order,
Closed his sojourn here below.

Seated with his brethren round
　him　　　　　　　　[met,
On the night when last they
For the law's complete fulfil-
　ment,
When the Lamb was duly ate,
Then before the twelve dis-
　ciples
For their food himself he set.

By a word the Word incarnate
　Simple bread to flesh divine,
Simple wine to blood con-
　verteth ;
But, if sense to doubt incline,
Under faith's sufficient teaching
Simple hearts all doubts re-
　sign.

For the remaining verses of this hymn, see 81, *Tantum ergo Sacramentum.*

Corpus Christi.

The Blessed Sacrament.

JESUS, my Lord, my God, my all!
   How can I love thee as I ought?
And how revere this wondrous gift,
   So far surpassing hope or thought?
     Sweet Sacrament, we thee adore,
     Oh make us love thee more and more.

Had I but Mary's sinless heart
   To love thee with, my dearest King,
Oh, with what bursts of fervent praise
   Thy goodness, Jesus, would I sing!
     Sweet Sacrament, we thee adore, etc.

Oh see! within a creature's hand
   The vast Creator deigns to be,
Reposing infant-like, as though
   On Joseph's arm, or Mary's knee.
     Sweet Sacrament, we thee adore, etc.

The Body, Soul, and Godhead, all,
   O mystery of love divine!
I cannot compass all I have,
   For all thou hast and art are mine.
     Sweet Sacrament, we thee adore, etc.

Sound, sound his praises higher still,
   And come, ye angels, to our aid;
'Tis God! 'tis God! the very God
   Whose power both men and angels made.
     Sweet Sacrament, we thee adore,
     Oh make us love thee more and more.

Corpus Christi.

The Holy Sacrifice.

When the Patriarch was returning
   Crowned with triumph from the fray,
Him the peaceful king of Salem
   Came to meet upon his way ;
Meekly bearing Bread and Wine,
Holy priesthood's awful sign.

On the truth thus dimly shadowed
   Later days a lustre shed ;
When the great High-Priest eternal,
   Under forms of Wine and Bread,
For the world's immortal food
Gave his Flesh and gave his Blood.

Wondrous gift !—The Word who fashioned
   All things by his might divine,
Bread into his Body changes,
   Into his own Blood the wine ;—
What though sense no change perceives,
Faith admires, adores, believes.

He who once to die a Victim
   On the cross did not refuse,
Day by day upon our altars,
   That same Sacrifice renews ;
Through his holy priesthood's hands,
Faithful to his last commands.

While the people all uniting
   In the Sacrifice sublime,
Offer Christ to his high Father,
   Offer up themselves with him ;
Then together with the priest
On the living Victim feast.

Sacred Heart of Jesus.

Summi Parentis Filio.

TO Christ, the Prince of peace,
 And Son of God most high,
The Father of the world to come,
 Sing we with holy joy.

Deep in his heart for us
 The wound of love he bore ;
That love, wherewith he still inflames
 The hearts that him adore.

O Jesu, victim blest,
 What else but love divine
Could thee constrain to open thus
 That sacred heart of thine ?

O fount of endless life,
 O spring of waters clear,
O flame celestial, cleansing all
 Who unto thee draw near.

Hide me in thy dear heart,
 For hither do I fly ;
There seek thy grace through life, in death
 Thine immortality.

Praise to the Father be,
 And sole-begotten Son ;
Praise, holy Paraclete, to thee,
 While endless ages run.

Sacred Heart of Jesus.

33

To Jesus' Heart.

TO Jesus' Heart, all burning
  With fervent love for men,
My heart with fondest yearning
  Shall raise its joyful strain.
    While ages course along,
    Blest be with loudest song
    The Sacred Heart of Jesus
    By every heart and tongue.

O Heart, for me on fire
  With love no man can speak,
My yet untold desire
  God gives me for thy sake.
    While ages course along,
    Blest be with loudest song
    The Sacred Heart of Jesus
    By every heart and tongue.

Too true I have forsaken
  Thy love by wilful sin ;
Yet now let me be taken
  Back by thy grace again.
    While ages course along,
    Blest be with loudest song
    The Sacred Heart of Jesus
    By every heart and tongue.

As thou art meek and lowly,
  And ever pure of heart,
So may my heart be wholly
  Of thine the counterpart.
    While ages course along,
    Blest be with loudest song
    The Sacred Heart of Jesus
    By every heart and tongue.

The Precious Blood.

Hail, Jesus, hail.

HAIL, Jesus, hail, who for my sake
    Sweet blood from Mary's veins didst take,
  And shed it all for me ;
Oh, blessed be my Saviour's blood,
My life, my light, my only good,
  To all eternity.

To endless ages let us praise
The precious blood, whose price could raise
  The world from wrath and sin ;
Whose streams our inward thirst appease,
And heal the sinner's worst disease,
  If he but bathe therein.

O sweetest blood, that can implore
Pardon of God, and heaven restore,
  The heaven which sin had lost :
While Abel's blood for vengeance pleads,
What Jesus shed still intercedes
  For those who wrong him most.

Oh, to be sprinkled from the wells
Of Christ's own sacred blood, excels
  Earth's best and highest bliss :
The ministers of wrath divine
Hurt not the happy hearts that shine
  With those red drops of his.

Ah, there is joy amid the saints,
And hell's despairing courage faints
  When this sweet song we raise :
Oh, louder then, and louder still,
Earth with one mighty chorus fill,
  The precious blood to praise.

To all the faithful who say or sing this hymn Pius VII. granted an indulgence of 100 days, applicable to the souls in purgatory.

Feasts of the B. V. Mary.

Ave maris stella.

Ave maris stella,
 Dei Mater alma,
Atque semper virgo,
 Felix cœli porta.

Sumens illud Ave
 Gabriélis ore,
Funda nos in pace,
 Mutans nomen Hevæ.

Solve vincla reis,
 Profer lumen cæcis,
Mala nostra pelle,
 Bona cuncta posce.

Monstra te esse matrem,
 Sumat per te preces,
Qui pro nobis natus,
 Tulit esse tuus.

Virgo singuláris,
 Inter omnes mitis,
Nos culpis solútos,
 Mites fac et castos.

Vitam præsta puram,
 Iter para tutum,
Ut vidéntes Jesum,
 Semper collætémur.

Sit laus Deó Patri,
 Summo Christo decus,
Spíritui sancto,
 Tribus honor unus.
  Amen.

Hail, thou Star of ocean,
 God's own Mother blest,
Ever-sinless Virgin,
 Gate of heavenly rest.

Taking that sweet Ave
 Which from Gabriel came,
Peace confirm within us,
 Changing Eva's name.

Break the captive's fetters,
 To the blind give day;
Chase all evils from us;
 For all blessings pray.

Show thyself a mother;
 May the Word divine,
Born for us thine Infant,
 Hear our prayers through thine.

Virgin all excelling,
 Mildest of the mild,
Freed from guilt, preserve us
 Meek and undefiled.

Keep our life all spotless,
 Make our way secure,
Till we find in Jesus
 Joy for evermore.

Praise to God the Father,
 Honour to the Son,
To the Holy Spirit
 Be the glory one.
  Amen.

Feasts of the B. V. Mary.

Daily, daily.

DAILY, daily, sing to Mary,
　Sing, my soul, her praises due ;
All her feasts, her actions worship
　With the heart's devotion true.
Lost in wondering contemplation,
　Be her majesty confest ;
Call her Mother, call her Virgin,
　Happy Mother, Virgin blest.

She is mighty to deliver ;
　Call her, trust her lovingly ;
When the tempest rages round thee,
　She will calm the troubled sea.
Gifts of heaven she has given,
　Noble lady, to our race :
She the Queen, who decks her subjects
　With the light of God's own grace.

Sing, my tongue, the Virgin's trophies,
　Who for us her Maker bore ;
For the curse of old inflicted,
　Peace and blessing to restore.
Sing in songs of praise unending,
　Sing the world's majestic Queen ;
Weary not, nor faint in telling
　All the gifts she gives to men.

All my senses, heart, affections,
　Strive to sound her glory forth ;
Spread abroad the sweet memorials
　Of the Virgin's priceless worth.
Where the voice of music thrilling,
　Where the tongue of eloquence,
That can utter hymns beseeming
　All her matchless excellence ?

Feasts of the B. V. Mary.

37

Hail, Queen of heaven.

HAIL, Queen of heaven, the ocean star,
   Guide of the wanderer here below,
Thrown on life's surge, we claim thy care,
   Save us from peril and from woe.
     Mother of Christ, Star of the sea,
     Pray for the wanderer, pray for me.

O gentle, chaste, and spotless Maid,
   We sinners make our prayers through thee ;
Remind thy Son that he has paid
   The price of our iniquity.
     Virgin, most pure, Star of the sea,
     Pray for the sinner, pray for me.

Sojourners in this vale of tears,
   To thee, blest Advocate, we cry,
Pity our sorrows, calm our fears,
   And soothe with hope our misery.
     Refuge in grief, Star of the sea,
     Pray for the mourner, pray for me.

And while to him who reigns above,
   In Godhead One, in persons Three,
The source of life, of grace, of love,
   Homage we pay on bended knee—
     Do thou, bright Queen, Star of the sea,
     Pray for thy children, pray for me.

Feasts of the B. V. Mary.

Look down, O Mother Mary.

LOOK down, O Mother Mary,
　　From thy bright throne above;
Cast down upon thy children
　　One only glance of love.
And if a heart so tender
　　With pity flows not o'er,
Then turn away, O Mother,
　　And look on us no more.

See how ungrateful sinners
　　We stand before thy Son;
His loving heart reproaches
　　The evil we have done.
But if thou wilt appease him,
　　Speak for us but one word;
Thou only canst obtain us
　　The pardon of our Lord.

O Mary, dearest Mother,
　　If thou wouldst have us live,
Say that we are thy children,
　　And Jesus will forgive.
Our sins make us unworthy
　　That title still to bear,
But thou art still our Mother;
　　Then show a mother's care.

Unfold to us thy mantle,
　　There stay we without fear:
What evil can befall us
　　If, Mother, thou art near?
O kindest, dearest Mother,
　　Thy sinful children save;
Look down on us with pity,
　　Who thy protection crave.

Feasts of the B. V. Mary.

Mother of Mercy.

MOTHER of mercy, day by day
   My love of thee grows more and more ;
Thy gifts are strewn upon my way
   Like sands upon the great sea-shore.

Though poverty and work and woe
   The masters of my life may be,
When times are worst, who does not know
   Darkness is light with love of thee ?

But scornful men have coldly said
   Thy love was leading me from God ;
And yet in this I did but tread
   The very path my Saviour trod.

They know but little of thy worth
   Who speak these heartless words to me ;
For what did Jesus love on earth
   One half so tenderly as thee ?

Get me the grace to love thee more ;
   Jesus will give if thou wilt plead ;
And, Mother, when life's cares are o'er,
   Oh I shall love thee then indeed.

Jesus, when his three hours were run,
   Bequeathed thee from the cross to me ;
And oh, how can I love thy Son,
   Sweet Mother, if I love not thee ?

Immaculate Conception.

O purest of creatures.

O PUREST of creatures, sweet Mother, sweet Maid,
   The one spotless womb wherein Jesus was laid !
Dark night hath come down on us, Mother, and we
Look out for thy shining, sweet Star of the sea !

Deep night hath come down on this rough-spoken world,
And the banners of darkness are boldly unfurled ;
And the tempest-tossed Church—all her eyes are on thee,
They look to thy shining, sweet Star of the sea !

The Church doth what God had first taught her to do ;
He looked o'er the world to find hearts that were true ;
Through the ages he looked, and he found none but thee,
And he loved thy clear shining, sweet Star of the sea !

He gazed on thy soul ; it was spotless and fair ;
For the empire of sin—it had never been there ;
None had e'er owned thee, dear Mother, but he,
And he blessed thy clear shining, sweet Star of the sea !

Earth gave him one lodging ; 'twas deep in thy breast,
And God found a home where the sinner finds rest ;
His home and his hiding-place both were in thee,
He was won by thy shining, sweet Star of the sea !

O blissful and calm was the wonderful rest
That thou gavest thy God in thy virginal breast ;
For the heaven he left, he found heaven in thee,
And he shone in thy shining, sweet Star of the sea !

Immaculate Conception.

41

Mary immaculate.

O MOTHER! I could weep for mirth,
   Joy fills my heart so fast;
My soul to-day is heaven on earth,
   Oh could the transport last!
     I think of thee, and what thou art,
      Thy majesty, thy state;
     And I keep singing in my heart,—
      Immaculate! Immaculate!

When Jesus looks upon thy face,
   His heart with rapture glows,
And in the Church, by his sweet grace,
   Thy blessed worship grows.
     I think of thee, and what thou art, etc.

The angels answer with their songs,
   Bright choirs in gleaming rows;
And saints flock round thy feet in throngs,
   And heaven with bliss o'erflows.
     I think of thee, and what thou art, etc.

Conceived, conceived Immaculate!
   Oh what a joy for thee!
Conceived, conceived Immaculate!
   Oh greater joy for me!
     I think of thee, and what thou art, etc.

It is this thought to-day that lifts
   My happy heart to heaven,
That for our sakes thy choicest gifts
   To thee, dear Queen, were given.
     I think of thee, and what thou art,
      Thy majesty, thy state;
     And I keep singing in my heart,—
      Immaculate! Immaculate!

Assumption.

Sing, sing, ye Angel bands.

SING, sing, ye Angel bands,
   All beautiful and bright:
For higher still, and higher,
   Through fields of starry light,
Mary, your Queen, ascends,
   Like the sweet moon at night.

A fairer flower than she
   On earth hath never been;
And, save the throne of God,
   Your heavens have never seen
A wonder half so bright
   As your ascending Queen.

O happy angels! look,
   How beautiful she is!
See! Jesus bears her up,
   Her hand is locked in his;
Oh who can tell the height
   Of that fair Mother's bliss?

And shall I lose thee then,
   Lose my sweet right to thee?
Ah, no—the angels' Queen
   Man's Mother still will be;
And thou, upon thy throne,
   Wilt keep thy love for me.

On, then, dear Pageant, on!
   Sweet music breathes around;
And love, like dew, distils
   On hearts in rapture bound;
The Queen of heaven goes up
   To be proclaimed and crowned!

Month of Mary.

Joy of my heart.

Joy of my heart! oh let me pay
    To thee thine own sweet month of May.
Mary, one gift I beg of thee,
My soul from sin and sorrow free.
Direct my wandering feet aright,
And be thyself mine own true light;
Be love of thee the purging fire,
To cleanse for God my heart's desire.
    Joy of my heart! oh let me pay
    To thee thine own sweet month of May.

Mary, make haste thy child to win
From sin and from the love of sin;
Thou, who wert pure as driven snow,
Make me as thou wert here below.
Write on my heart's most secret core
The five dear wounds that Jesus bore.
Oh give me tears to shed with thee
Beneath the cross on Calvary.
    Joy of my heart! etc.

O Queen of Heaven! obtain for me
Thy glory there one day to see.
Oh then and there, on that bright day,
To me thy womb's chaste Fruit display.
One more request and I have done;—
With love of thee and thy dear Son,
More let me burn, and more each day,
Till love of self is burned away.
    Joy of my heart! etc.

Month of Mary.

Our Lady's Image.

THIS is the image of our Queen
  Who reigns in bliss above,
Of her who is the hope of men,
  Whom men and angels love.
Most holy Mary, at thy feet
  I bend a suppliant knee;
In this thy own sweet month of May,
  Pray thou to God for me.

The sacred homage that we pay
  To Mary's image here,
To Mary's self, then on to God
  Ascends the starry sphere.
Most holy Mary, at thy feet
  I bend a suppliant knee;
In this thy own sweet month of May,
  Pray thou to God for me.

Sweet are the flowers we have culled
  This image to adorn,
But sweeter far is Mary's self,
  That rose without a thorn.
Most holy Mary, at thy feet
  I bend a suppliant knee;
In this thy own sweet month of May,
  Pray thou to God for me.

O Lady, by the stars that make
  A glory round thy head,
And by thy pure uplifted hands
  That for thy children plead,
When at the Judgment-seat I stand,
  And my dread Saviour see,
When hell is raging for my soul,
  Pray thou to God for me.

The Holy Rosary,

Victorious over sin and unbelief.

THE clouds hang thick o'er Israel's camp
   As dawns the battle day,
Arise! bright star of Dominic,
   And chase the gloom away:
And where the foemen fiercest press
   Thy radiance let us see;
Shine o'er the banners of thy sons,
   And lead to victory.

The weapon which our father gave
   Each hand shall fearless wield:
Who bear our Lady's Rosary
   Need neither sword nor shield:
With dauntless faith the ranks they face
   Of error and of sin,
And, armed with those blest beads alone,
   The victory they win.

See o'er Lepanto's waters spread
   The Moslem's dark array:
A Voice to Christendom went forth,
   And gave the word to pray:
Jesus and Mary! names of strength
   Invoked, and not in vain;
They conquered in the hour of need,
   And conquer shall again.

As Pius then to Europe spake,
   So Leo speaks once more;
The Rosary our weapon still,
   To wield in holy war:
Ave Maria! from each tongue
   Shall rise the pleading word;
Oh doubt not that the prayer of faith
   Will now, as then, be heard.

The Holy Rosary.

To our Lady of the Rosary.

QUEEN of the Holy Rosary!
  Oh bless us as we pray,
And offer thee our roses
  In garlands day by day;
While from our Father's garden,
  With loving hearts and bold,
We gather to thine honour
  Buds white, and red, and gold.

Queen of the Holy Rosary!
  Each mystery blends with thine
The sacred life of Jesus
  In every step divine.
Thy soul was his fair garden,
  Thy virgin breast his throne,
Thy thoughts his faithful mirror
  Reflecting him alone.

Sweet Lady of the Rosary!
  White roses let us bring,
And lay them round thy footstool
  Before our Infant King.
For nestling in thy bosom
  God's Son was fain to be,
The child of thy obedience
  And spotless purity.

Dear Lady of the Rosary!
  Red roses cast we down;
But let thy fingers weave them
  Into a worthy crown.
For how can we poor sinners
  Do aught but weep with thee,
When in thy train we follow
  Our God to Calvary?

Queen of the Holy Rosary!
  What radiancy of love,
What splendour and what glory
  Surround thy court above!
Oh, in thy tender pity,
  Dear source of love untold,
Refuse not this our offering,
  Our flowers white, red, and gold.

The Holy Rosary.

Joyful Mysteries.

1. The Annunciation—Humility.

HAIL, full of grace and purity,
  Meek Handmaid of the Lord ;
Hail, model of *humility*,
  Chaste Mother of the Word.

2. The Visitation—Charity.

By that pure love which prompted thee
  To seek thy cousin blest,
Pray that the fires of *charity*
  May burn within our breast.

3. The Birth of our Lord—Poverty.

This blessing beg, O Virgin Queen,
  From Jesus through his birth,
By holy *poverty* to wean
  Our hearts from things of earth.

4. The Presentation of our Lord—Obedience.

Most holy Virgin, Maiden mild,
  Obtain for us, we pray,
To imitate thy Holy Child
  By striving *to obey.*

5. The Finding of our Lord—Love of his service.

By thy dear Son, restored to thee,
  This grace for us implore,
To *serve our Lord* more faithfully,
  And love him more and more.

Concluding verse.

Queen of the Holy Rosary,
  With tender love look down,
And bless the hearts that offer thee
  This chaplet for thy crown.

The Holy Rosary.

Sorrowful Mysteries.

1. *The Agony of our Lord—Prayer.*

LORD, by thy prayer in agony
   On Olivet alone,
Teach us *to pray*, resigned like thee,
   And say "Thy will be done."

2. *The Scourging—Mortification.*

Sweet Saviour, who didst bear for me
   The scourge's pain intense,
Help me to fly all luxury,
   And *mortify* each sense.

3. *The Crowning with Thorns—Fortitude.*

By the sharp thorns so meekly borne,
   And scoffs and buffets rude,
Teach us to bear all pain and scorn
   With holy *fortitude*.

4. *The Carrying of the Cross—Patience.*

Lord, by thy cross thy people spare,
   And on us pity take,
Help us our daily cross to bear
   With *patience* for thy sake.

5. *The Crucifixion—Self-sacrifice.*

O Jesus, victim for man's fall,
   Lamb slain on Calvary,
Accept henceforth our lives, our all,
   In *sacrifice* to thee.

Concluding verse.

Queen of the Holy Rosary,
   With tender love look down,
And bless the hearts that offer thee
   This chaplet for thy crown.

The Holy Rosary.

Glorious Mysteries.

1. *The Resurrection—Faith.*

ALL hail, great Conqueror, to thee,
   Arisen from the dead !
Grant us the light of *faith*, that we
   May in thy footsteps tread.

2. *The Ascension—Hope.*

To heaven thou dost ascend again,
   Sweet Saviour of our race,
With *hope* our fainting hearts sustain
   To see in heaven thy face.

3. *The Descent of the Holy Ghost—Zeal for Souls.*

O Holy Ghost, who didst descend
   In cloven tongues of fire,
Our souls, which all too earthward tend,
   With burning *zeal* inspire.

4. *The Assumption—Devotion to our Lady.*

Mother of God, enthroned above,
   Beseech thy Son anew,
To fill our hearts with childlike *love*
   For thee our Mother too.

5. *The Coronation of our Lady—Perseverance.*

All-gracious Queen of Angels, deign
   Our last request to hear,
For us this crowning gift obtain—
   The grace to *persevere*.

Concluding verse.

Queen of the Holy Rosary,
   With tender love look down,
And bless the hearts that offer thee
   This chaplet for thy crown.

Angel Guardian.

Dear Angel, ever at my side.

DEAR Angel, ever at my side,
   How loving must thou be,
To leave thy home in heaven to guard
   A guilty wretch like me.

Thy beautiful and shining face
   I see not, though so near;
The sweetness of thy soft low voice
   I am too deaf to hear.

But I have felt thee in my thoughts
   Fighting with sin for me;
And when my heart loves God, I know
   The sweetness is from thee.

And when, dear Spirit, I kneel down,
   Morning and night, to prayer,
Something there is within my heart
   Which tells me thou art there.

Yes, when I pray thou prayest too,
   Thy prayer is all for me;
But when I sleep, thou sleepest not,
   But watchest patiently.

Then, for thy sake, dear Angel, now
   More humble will I be:
But I am weak; and when I fall,
   Oh weary not of me.

Oh weary not, but love me still,
   For Mary's sake, thy Queen;
She never tired of me, though I
   Her worst of sons have been.

Then love me, love me, Angel dear,
   And I will love thee more;
And help me when my soul is cast
   Upon the eternal shore.

St. Joseph.

51

Hail! holy Joseph, hail!

HAIL! holy Joseph, hail!
  Husband of Mary, hail!
Chaste as the lily flower
In Eden's peaceful vale.

Hail! holy Joseph, hail!
Father of Christ esteemed,
Father be thou to those
Thy Foster-Son redeemed.

Hail! holy Joseph, hail!
Prince of the house of God,
May his best graces be
By thy sweet hands bestowed.

Hail! holy Joseph, hail!
Comrade of angels, hail!
Cheer thou the hearts that faint,
And guide the steps that fail.

Hail! holy Joseph, hail!
God's choice wert thou alone;
To thee the Word made flesh
Was subject as a Son.

Hail! holy Joseph, hail!
Teach us our flesh to tame;
And, Mary, keep the hearts
That love thy husband's name.

Mother of Jesus! bless,
And bless, ye saints on high,
All meek and simple souls
That to Saint Joseph cry.

St. Joseph.

52

Patronage of St. Joseph.

DEAR Husband of Mary! dear Nurse of her Child!
  Life's ways are full weary, the desert is wild;
Bleak sands are all round us, no home can we see;
Sweet Spouse of our Lady, we lean upon thee.

For thou to the pilgrim art father and guide,
And Jesus and Mary felt safe by thy side;
Ah blessed Saint Joseph, how safe I should be,
Sweet Spouse of our Lady, if thou wert with me!

O blessed Saint Joseph! how great was thy worth,
The one chosen shadow of God upon earth,
The Father of Jesus—ah then wilt thou be,
Sweet Spouse of our Lady, a father to me?

Thou hast not forgotten the long dreary road,
When Mary took turns with thee bearing thy God;
Yet light was that burden, none lighter could be:
Sweet Spouse of our Lady, oh canst thou bear me?

When the treasures of God were unsheltered on earth,
Safe keeping was found for them both in thy worth;
O Father of Jesus, be father to me,
Sweet Spouse of our Lady, and I will love thee.

God chose thee for Jesus and Mary—wilt thou
Forgive a poor exile for choosing thee now?
There is no saint in heaven I worship like thee,
Sweet Spouse of our Lady, oh deign to love me!

SS. Peter and Paul.

53

Decora lux æternitatis auream.

IT is no earthly summer's ray
    That sheds this golden brightness round,
Crowning with heavenly light the day
    The Princes of the Church were crowned.

The blessed seer, to whom was given
    The hearts of men to teach and school,
And he that keeps the keys of heaven,
    For those on earth that own his rule,—

Fathers of mighty Rome, whose word
    Shall pass the doom of life or death,
By humble cross and bleeding sword
    Well have they won their laurel wreath.

O happy Rome, made holy now
    By these two martyrs' glorious blood;
Earth's best and fairest cities bow,
    By thy superior claims subdued.

For thou alone art worth them all,
    City of martyrs! thou alone
Canst cheer our pilgrim hearts, and call
    The Saviour's sheep to Peter's throne.

All honour, power, and praise be given
    To him who reigns in bliss on high,
For endless, endless years in heaven,
    One only God in Trinity.

St. Dominic.

Novus athleta Domini.

SOUND the mighty champion's praises,
    Raise the song for him who came
Charged to tell the Gospel tidings,
    Charged to spread the Gospel flame—
        Lordly errand,
    Suiting well his lordly name.

Stainless as a virgin lily,
    Fervent as a flaming brand,
Lo, he flies, still onward speeding,
    Flies to do his Lord's command—
        Flies to rescue
    Captive souls from Satan's hand.

Treading down this world of evil,
    To his mighty task he goes;
Stript of all, he seeks the conflict,
    Turns him to Christ's banded foes—
        Grace sustaining
    With the fire that inward glows.

Lo, his arms of heavenly temper—
    Words and signs of wondrous power,
Prayers of love, and tears of pity,
    Whilst his warrior children bore
        His commission
    Onward still from shore to shore.

Sing we to the Triune Godhead,
    Honour, glory, power, and praise;
May be at our father's pleading,
    Deign his children's souls to raise,
        Cleansed and perfect,
    To his reign of endless days.

St. Dominic,

Preacher of the Rosary.

THOU who, hero-like, hast striven
    For the cause of God and heaven,
Dominic, whose life was given
        Sinners to recall,
Saint of high and dauntless spirit,
By thy vast unmeasured merit,
By thy name which we inherit,
        Hear us when we call.

Flower of chastity, the fairest
Of her lily buds thou bearest
Snow-white as the robe thou wearest,
        Gift from hands divine.
With thy brow of starry splendour,
With thine eyes so mild and tender,
Mary's client, truth's defender,
        To our prayers incline.

Great apostle, ever claiming
Souls for Jesus, by the naming
Mary and her Son proclaiming
        Mysteries of faith.
Still, O Dominic, the preaching
Of those childlike beads is reaching
Childlike hearts, all sweetly teaching
        Christ's own life and death.

With those Aves, first and plainest
Of the Church's prayers, thou rainest
Blessings on the earth, and gainest
        Souls whom Jesus made.
Loving Father, at thy station
Of seraphic contemplation,
In each hour of dark temptation
        Give thy saving aid.

St. George.

Deus tuorum militum.

O THOU, of all thy warriors Lord,
    Thyself the crown and sure reward;
Set us from sinful fetters free,
Who sing thy martyr's victory.

In selfish pleasures' worldly round
The taste of bitter gall he found;
But sweet to him was thy dear Name,
And so to heavenly joys he came.

Right manfully his cross he bore,
And ran his race of torments sore;
For thee he poured his life away;
With thee he lives in endless day.

We, then, before thee bending low,
Intreat thee, Lord, thy love to show
On this the day thy martyr died,
Who in thy saints are glorified.

To God the Father, with the Son,
And Holy Spirit, Three in One,
Be praise and glory evermore,
As in th' eternity before.

This Hymn may be used on the festival of any martyr.

St. Patrick.

57

Hail, glorious St. Patrick.

HAIL, glorious Saint Patrick, dear Saint of our isle!
   On us, thy poor children, bestow a sweet smile;
And now thou art high in the mansions above,
On Erin's green valleys look down in thy love.

Hail, glorious Saint Patrick, thy words were once strong
Against Satan's wiles and a heretic throng;
Not less in thy might where in heaven thou art,
Oh, come to our aid, in our battle take part.

In the war against sin, in the fight for the faith,
Dear Saint, may thy children resist to the death;
May their strength be in meekness, in penance, and prayer,
Their banner the cross, which they glory to bear.

Thy people, now exiles on many a shore,
Shall love and revere thee till time be no more,
And the fire thou hast kindled shall ever burn bright,
Its warmth undiminished, undying its light.

Ever bless and defend the sweet land of our birth,
Where the shamrock still blooms as when thou wert on earth,
And our hearts shall yet burn wheresoever we roam,
For God and Saint Patrick and our native home.

St. Thomas Aquinas,

Patron of the Angelic Warfare.

FLOWER of innocence, Saint Thomas,
   Unto thee our hearts we raise,
Patron of our holy warfare,
   Hear our humble hymn of praise.
Chosen lily, virgin Doctor,
   Teach us how to follow thee,
Spotless lamb, to Jesus guide us
   In our robes of purity.

Aid us in our ceaseless warfare,
   War angelic against sin;
Shield us from the wily tempter,
   Pray for us that we may win.
Save our souls from ill,—frail vessels
   Tossing on temptation's sea;
Guide them safely to the haven
   Of a blest eternity.

Soul unspotted, rendered worthy,
   In thy lofty vision's flight,
Deepest mysteries to fathom
   By the Paraclete's keen light;
Teach us now by thine example
   How to choose the better part,
Seeking out the truths unfolded
   Only to the clean of heart.

Pressing onwards through life's journey,
   We thy sacred girdle wear;
Let it be to us the token
   Of thy ever-watchful care:
By thy matchless virtue keep us
   From all sinful pleasures free,
That in heaven we too may merit
   Crowns of spotless chastity.

St. Mary Magdalen,

Model of Penitents.

Once a very sinful woman
  Came our blessed Lord to meet;
Struck at once with pain and sorrow,
  Down she sank before his feet,
Bathed them with her tears of penance,
  Wiped them with her hair, and then
Heard her Saviour's words of pardon:
  Blessed Mary Magdalen!

From that happy day of mercy
  She was ever near our Lord,
Nourishing her soul with wisdom,
  Listening to his saving word.
May my sinful soul, forgiven,
  Never more fall back again,
Strengthened by thy sweet example,
  Holy Mary Magdalen!

On the cross, her sins redeeming,
  She beheld our Saviour die;
There she stood, all broken-hearted,
  With his blessed Mother nigh.
When at last he rose triumphant,
  Joy of angels and of men,
Who was first to see him risen?
  Holy Mary Magdalen!

Years she spent in happy penance,
  Loving with undying love,
Praying, hoping, sweetly sighing,
  Till she passed to heaven above.
I will love and serve my Saviour
  Till my heavenly crown I gain;
Make me love him for his mercy,
  Holy Mary Magdalen!

St. Catherine of Siena.

O Spouse of Christ.

O SPOUSE of Christ, on whom
   His choicest love was laid,
The spousals of the saints were thine,
   In woe and suffering made.

Around thy virgin brow
   A thorny radiance shines,
And brightly from thy wounded hands
   The living glory shines.

Above thee from thy birth
   Hovered the mystic Dove,
Thy life—a seraph's life on earth—
   Closed with a death of love.

O Mother, who on earth
   Didst conquer by thy prayers,
Regard us as thy children now,
   And through the eternal years.

Glory to God on high,
   To Father and to Son,
And Holy Spirit, Lord of Life,
   Eternal Three in One.

All Saints.

61

Placare, Christe, servulis.

O CHRIST, thy guilty people spare;
    Lo, kneeling at thy gracious throne,
Thy Virgin Mother pours her prayer,
    Imploring pardon for her own.

Ye Angels, happy evermore,
    Who in your circles nine ascend,
As ye have guarded us before,
    So still from harm our steps defend.

Ye Prophets, and Apostles high,
    Behold our penitential tears;
And plead for us when death is nigh,
    And our all-searching Judge appears.

Ye Martyrs all, a purple band,
    And Confessors, a white-robed train;
Oh, call us to our native land,
    From this our exile, back again.

And ye, O choirs of Virgins chaste,
    Receive us to your seats on high;
With Hermits whom the desert waste
    Sent up of old into the sky.

Drive from the flock, O Spirits blest,
    The false and faithless race away;
That all within one fold may rest
    Secure beneath one shepherd's sway.

To God the Father glory be,
    And to his sole-begotten Son:
And glory, Holy Ghost, to thee
    While everlasting ages run.

Also **74.**

All Souls.

62

Psalm 129.

DE profúndis clamávi ad te, Dómine: * Dómine, exáudi vocem meam.
2. Fiant aures tuæ inténtes: * in vocem deprecatiónis meæ.
3. Si iniquitátes observáveris, Dómine: * Dómine, quis sustinébit?
4. Quia apud te propitiátio est: * et propter legem tuam sustínui te, Dómine.
5. Sustínuit ánima mea in verbo ejus: * sperávit ánima mea in Dómino.
6. A custódia matutína usque ad noctem: * speret Israel in Dómino.
7. Quia apud Dóminum misericórdia: * et copiósa apud eum redémptio.
8. Et ipse rédimet Israel: * ex ómnibus iniquitátibus ejus.

Réquiem ætérnam dona eis Dómine; et lux perpétua lúceat eis.

OUT of the depths have I cried unto thee, O Lord: Lord, hear my voice.
O let thine ears consider well: the voice of my supplication.
If thou, O Lord, wilt mark iniquities: Lord, who shall abide it?
For with thee there is merciful forgiveness: and because of thy law, I have waited for thee, O Lord.
My soul hath waited on his word: my soul hath hoped in the Lord.
From the morning watch even until night: let Israel hope in the Lord.
For with the Lord, there is mercy: and with him is plenteous redemption.
And he shall redeem Israel: from all his iniquities.

Eternal rest give to them, O Lord; and let perpetual light shine upon them.

All Souls.

To our Lady of the Holy Souls.

OH, turn to Jesus, Mother, turn,
    And call him by his tenderest names;
Pray for the holy souls that burn
    This hour amid the cleansing flames.

Ah, they have fought a gallant fight;
    In death's cold arms they persevered;
And after life's uncheery night
    The harbour of their rest is neared.

In pains beyond all earthly pains,
    Favourites of Jesus, there they lie,
Letting the fire wear out their stains,
    And worshipping God's purity.

They are the children of thy tears;
    Then hasten, Mother, to their aid;
In pity think each hour appears
    An age while glory is delayed.

O Mary, let thy Son no more
    His lingering spouses thus expect;
God's children to their God restore,
    And to the Spirit his elect.

Pray, then, as thou hast ever prayed;
    Angels and souls, all look to thee;
God waits thy prayers, for he hath made
    Those prayers his law of charity.

Missions and Retreats.

Hail, holy Mission.

HAIL! holy Mission, hail!
  Sighing we turn to thee,
For weary have we found
  The path of sin to be.

Hail! holy Mission, hail!
  Sent to us from above;
When Jesus with his Cross
  Comes to win back our love.

Hail! holy Mission, hail!
  Time of repentant tears;
When to the soul returns
  The peace of former years.

Hail! holy Mission, hail!
  Sweet time of humble prayer;
When rests the soul on God,
  Freed from this dark world's care.

Hail! holy Mission, hail!
  Time of all others blest;
When in the loving soul,
  Jesus takes up his rest.

Hail! holy Mission, hail!
  Foretaste of joys above:
O Jesus, make our hearts
  Burn with thy tender love.

Missions and Retreats.

65

Invitation to the Sinner.

OH, come to the merciful Saviour that calls you,
   Oh, come to the Lord who forgives and forgets ;
Though dark be the fortune on earth that befalls you,
   There's a bright home above, where the sun never sets.

Oh come, then, to Jesus whose arms are extended
   To fold his dear children in closest embrace :
Oh come, for your exile will shortly be ended,
   And Jesus will show you his beautiful face.

Then come to the Saviour, whose mercy grows brighter
   The longer you look at the depth of his love ;
And fear not, 'tis Jesus, and life's cares grow lighter
   As you think of the home and the glory above.

Have you sinned as none else in the world have before you?
   Are you blacker than all other creatures in guilt?
Oh fear not, oh fear not, the mother that bore you
   Loves you less than the Saviour whose blood you have spilt.

Oh come, then, to Jesus and say how you love him,
   And swear at his feet you will keep in his grace ;
For one tear that is shed by a sinner can move him,
   And your sins will drop off in his tender embrace.

Then come to his feet, and lay open your story
   Of suffering and sorrow, of guilt and of shame ;
For the pardon of sin is the crown of his glory,
   And the joy of our Lord to be true to his name.

Missions and Retreats.

66

Hymn of Repentant Sorrow.

JESUS, my God, behold at length the time,
   When I resolve to turn away from crime.
Oh pardon me, Jesus, thy mercy I implore,
I will never more offend thee—
Oh pardon me, Jesus, thy mercy I implore,
I will never more offend thee—no, never more.

Since my poor soul thy precious blood hath cost,
Suffer me not for ever to be lost.
Oh pardon me, Jesus, thy mercy I implore,
I will never more offend thee —
Oh pardon me, Jesus, thy mercy I implore,
I will never more offend thee—no, never more.

Kneeling in tears, behold me at thy feet,
Like Magdalen, forgiveness I entreat.
Oh pardon me, Jesus, thy mercy I implore,
I will never more offend thee—
Oh pardon me, Jesus, thy mercy I implore,
I will never more offend thee—no, never more.

Missions and Retreats.

67

Act of Contrition.

GOD of mercy and compassion,
  Look with pity upon me.
Father, let me call thee Father,
  'Tis thy child returns to thee.
    Jesus, Lord, I ask for mercy;
      Let me not implore in vain;
    All my sins—I now detest them,
      Never will I sin again.

By my sins I have deserved
  Death and endless misery;
Hell, with all its pains and torments,
  And for all eternity.
    Jesus, Lord, I ask for mercy;
      Let me not implore in vain;
    All my sins—I now detest them,
      Never will I sin again.

By my sins I have abandoned
  Right and claim to heaven above;
Where the saints rejoice for ever,
  In a boundless sea of love.
    Jesus, Lord, I ask for mercy;
      Let me not implore in vain;
    All my sins—I now detest them,
      Never will I sin again.

See our Saviour, bleeding, dying,
  On the Cross of Calvary;
To that Cross my sins have nailed him,
  Yet he bleeds and dies for me.
    Jesus, Lord, I ask for mercy;
      Let me not implore in vain;
    All my sins—I now detest them,
      Never will I sin again.

Occasional.

The Eternal Father.

MY God, how wonderful thou art,
   Thy Majesty how bright,
How beautiful thy mercy-seat
   In depths of burning light!

How dread are thine eternal years,
   O everlasting Lord,
By prostrate spirits day and night
   Incessantly adored!

How beautiful, how beautiful
   The sight of thee must be,
Thine endless wisdom, boundless power,
   And awful purity!

Oh how I fear thee, living God!
   With deepest, tenderest fears,
And worship thee with trembling hope
   And penitential tears.

Yet I may love thee too, O Lord!
   Almighty as thou art;
For thou hast stooped to ask of me
   The love of my poor heart.

No earthly father loves like thee,
   No mother half so mild
Bears and forbears, as thou hast done
   With me thy sinful child.

Only to sit and think of God,
   Oh what a joy it is!
To think the thought, to breathe the Name,
   Earth has no higher bliss!

Father of Jesus, love's Reward,
   What rapture will it be,
Prostrate before thy Throne to lie,
   And gaze and gaze on thee!

Occasional.

The Will of God.

I WORSHIP thee, sweet Will of God,
   And all thy ways adore;
And every day I live I seem
   To love thee more and more.

Thou wert the end, the blessed rule
   Of Jesu's toils and tears:
Thou wert the passion of his heart
   Those three-and-thirty years.

And he hath breathed into my soul
   A special love of thee,
A love to lose my will in his,
   And by that loss be free.

I love to kiss each print where thou
   Hast set thine unseen feet:
I cannot fear thee, blessed Will,
   Thine empire is so sweet.

I know not what it is to doubt,
   My heart is ever gay;
I run no risk, for come what will
   Thou always hast thy way.

I have no cares, O blessed Will,
   For all my cares are thine;
I live in triumph, Lord, for thou
   Hast made thy triumph mine.

He always wins who sides with God,
   To him no chance is lost;
God's will is sweetest to him when
   It triumphs at his cost.

Ill that he blesses is our good,
   And unblest good is ill;
And all is right that seems most wrong,
   If it be his sweet Will.

Occasional.

70

Hymn of St. Francis Xavier.

MY God, I love thee, not because
   I hope for heaven thereby ;
Nor yet because who love thee not
   Must burn eternally.

Thou, O my Jesus, thou didst me
   Upon the cross embrace ;
For me didst bear the nails and spear,
   And manifold disgrace ;

And griefs and torments numberless,
   And sweat of agony ;
E'en death itself—and all for one
   Who was thine enemy.

Then why, O blessed Jesu Christ,
   Should I not love thee well ;
Not for the sake of winning heaven,
   Or of escaping hell ;

Not with the hope of gaining aught,
   Not seeking a reward ;
But, as thyself has lovèd me,
   O ever-loving Lord ?

E'en so I love thee, and will love,
   And in thy praise will sing,
Solely because thou art my God
   And my eternal King.

Occasional.

71

Jesus is God.

JESUS is God ; the solid earth,
 The ocean broad and bright,
The countless stars, like golden dust
 That strew the skies at night,
The wheeling storm, the dreadful fire,
 The pleasant wholesome air,
The summer's sun, the winter's frost,
 His own creations were.

Jesus is God ; the glorious bands
 Of golden angels sing
Songs of adoring praise to him,
 Their Maker and their King :
He was true God in Bethlehem's crib,
 On Calvary's cross true God,
He who in heaven eternal reigned,
 In time on earth abode.

Jesus is God ; alas, they say
 On earth the numbers grow
Who his divinity blaspheme
 To their unfailing woe :
And yet, what is the single end
 Of this life's mortal span,
Except to glorify the God
 Who for our sakes was Man ?

Jesus is God ; let sorrow come
 And pain and every ill ;
All are worth while—for all are means
 His glory to fulfil ;
Worth while a thousand years of life
 To speak one little word,
If by our Credo we might own
 The Godhead of our Lord.

Occasional.

72

Jesus, my God and my all.

O JESUS, Jesus, dearest Lord,
   Forgive me if I say
For very love thy sacred name
   A thousand times a day.

I love thee so, I know not how
   My transports to control;
Thy love is like a burning fire
   Within my very soul.

Oh wonderful, that thou shouldst let
   So vile a heart as mine
Love thee with such a love as this,
   And make so free with thine.

For thou to me art all in all,
   My honour and my wealth,
My heart's desire, my body's strength,
   My soul's eternal health.

What limit is there to thee, love?
   Thy flight where wilt thou stay?
On, on, our Lord is sweeter far
   To-day than yesterday.

O love of Jesus, blessed love,
   So will it ever be;
Time cannot hold thy wondrous growth,
   No, nor eternity.

Occasional.

73

Pilgrims of the Night.

HARK, hark, my soul, angelic songs are swelling
   O'er earth's green fields and ocean's wave-beat shore ;
How sweet the truth those blessed strains are telling
   Of that new life where sin shall be no more.
      Angels of Jesus ; angels of light,
      Singing to welcome the pilgrims of the night.

Darker than night life's shadows fall around us,
   And like benighted men we miss our mark ;
God hides himself, and grace hath scarcely found us,
   Ere death finds out his victims in the dark.
      Angels of Jesus ; angels of light, etc.

Onward we go, for still we hear them singing,
   'Come, weary souls, for Jesus bids you come ;'
And through the dark, its echoes sweetly ringing,
   The music of the gospel leads us home.
      Angels of Jesus ; angels of light, etc.

Far, far away, like bells at evening pealing,
   The voice of Jesus sounds o'er land and sea ;
And laden souls, by thousands meekly stealing,
   Kind Shepherd, turn their weary steps to thee.
      Angels of Jesus ; angels of light, etc.

Rest comes at length : though life be long and dreary,
   The day must dawn, and darksome night be past ;
All journeys end in welcomes to the weary,
   And heaven, the heart's true home, will come at last.
      Angels of Jesus ; angels of light, etc.

Angels, sing on, your faithful watches keeping,
   Sing us sweet fragments of the songs above ;
While we toil on, and soothe ourselves with weeping,
   Till life's long night shall break in endless love.
      Angels of Jesus ; angels of light,
      Singing to welcome the pilgrims of the night.

Occasional.

74

Paradise.

O PARADISE! O Paradise!
    Who doth not crave for rest?
Who would not seek the happy land
    Where they that loved are blest;
Where loyal hearts and true
    Stand ever in the light,
All rapture through and through
    In God's most holy sight?

O Paradise! O Paradise!
    'Tis weary waiting here;
I long to be where Jesus is,
    To feel, to see him near;
        Where loyal hearts, etc.

O Paradise! O Paradise!
    I want to sin no more;
I want to be as pure on earth
    As on thy spotless shore;
        Where loyal hearts, etc.

O Paradise! O Paradise!
    I greatly long to see
The special place my dearest Lord
    Is furnishing for me;
        Where loyal hearts, etc.

O Paradise! O Paradise!
    I feel 'twill not be long;
Patience! I almost think I hear
    Faint fragments of thy song;
Where loyal hearts and true
    Stand ever in the light,
All rapture through and through
    In God's most holy sight!

Occasional.

75

The Soldiers of Christ.

HARK! the sound of the fight hath gone forth,
    And we must not tarry at home;
For our Lord from the south and the north
    Has commanded his soldiers to come.
We must on with our banner unfurled;
    We must on: it is Jesus who leads;
We must hasten to conquer the world
    With the sign of the Lamb who bleeds.

We must stand to our colours like men;
    Our Lord is a leader to love;
For the wounded he heals, and the slain
    He crowns in his city above.
We must march to the battle with speed,
    Upon earth our one duty is strife;
Oh blest are the soldiers who bleed
    For the Saviour who died to give life!

There is Jesus in heaven above,
    There is Jesus on earth below,
And his the one standard we love,
    And his the one watchword we know.
Let us sing the new song of the Lamb;
    Let us sing round our banner so brave;
Let us sing of that beautiful Blood
    That was shed to redeem and to save.

Occasional.

Faith of our Fathers.

FAITH of our Fathers! living still,
    In spite of dungeon, fire, and sword;
Oh how our hearts beat high with joy
    Whene'er we hear that glorious word:
        Faith of our Fathers! holy Faith!
        We will be true to thee till death.

Our Fathers chained in prisons dark
    Were still in heart and conscience free;
How sweet would be their children's fate,
    If they like them could die for thee!
        Faith of our Fathers! holy Faith!
        We will be true to thee till death.

Faith of our Fathers! Mary's prayers
    Shall win our country back to thee;
And through the truth that comes from God,
    England shall then indeed be free.
        Faith of our Fathers! holy Faith!
        We will be true to thee till death.

Faith of our Fathers! we will love
    Both friend and foe in all our strife:
And preach thee too, as love knows how,
    By kindly words and virtuous life.
        Faith of our Fathers! holy Faith!
        We will be true to thee till death.

Evening.

77

Christe, qui lux es, et dies.

O CHRIST, thou brightness of the day
 That chaseth night's dull shades away,
Thou splendour of thy Father's light
That show'st his glories to our sight:
  We meekly pray thee, holy Lord,
   Defend us through the nightly hours;
  Thou canst a holy rest accord,
   Grant that such holy rest be ours.

Drive far the heavy sleep of sin,
Lest the untiring foe steal in;
And with his foul and deadly guile
The weak consenting flesh defile:
  Grant while our eyes are closed in sleep
   Our hearts may ever watch to thee,
  And let thine arm securely keep
   Each one of thy dear family.

Our sole defence, watch o'er us still
To guard from all the powers of ill;
Rule thou o'er us, O King of heaven,
For whom thy blood was freely given:
  Be mindful of us, Lord, while we
   This dull and fleshly burden bear,
  And let our souls still find in thee,
   A sweet defence for ever near.

Mother of love and mercy mild,
Mother of graces undefiled,
Drive back the foe, and to thy Son
Conduct our souls when life is done:
  Glory to thee, our Saviour sweet,
   Born of a spotless Mother-maid;
  To Father and to Paraclete
   Like glory be for ever paid.

Evening.

78

Sweet Saviour, bless us.

SWEET Saviour, bless us ere we go;
　Thy word into our minds instil;
And make our lukewarm hearts to glow
　With lowly love and fervent will.
Through life's long day and death's dark night,
　O gentle Jesus, be our light.

The day is done; its hours have run;
　And thou hast taken count of all—
The scanty triumphs grace hath won,
　The broken vow, the frequent fall.
Through life's long day and death's dark night,
　O gentle Jesus, be our light.

Grant us, dear Lord, from evil ways
　True absolution and release;
And bless us more than in past days
　With purity and inward peace.
Through life's long day and death's dark night,
　O gentle Jesus, be our light.

Do more than pardon; give us joy,
　Sweet fear and sober liberty,
And loving hearts without alloy,
　That only long to be like thee.
Through life's long day and death's dark night,
　O gentle Jesus, be our light.

Sweet Saviour, bless us; night is come,
　Mary and Joseph near us be;
Good angels watch about our home;
　And we are one day nearer thee.
Through life's long day and death's dark night,
　O gentle Jesus, be our light.

Benediction of the Most Holy Sacrament.

79

O Salutaris Hostia.

O SALUTARIS hóstia,
   Quæ cœli pandis óstium:
Bella premunt hostília,
Da robur, fer auxílium.

Uni trinóque Dómino
Sit sempitérna gloria,
Qui vitam sine término
Nobis donet in pátria.
             Amen.

O SAVING Victim, opening wide [below!
   The gate of heaven to man
Our foes press on from every side;
   Thine aid supply, thy strength bestow.

To thy great name be endless praise,
   Immortal Godhead, one in three. [days
O grant us endless length of
In our true native land with thee. Amen.

The Litany of the Blessed Virgin usually follows, or one of Nos. 82 to 86. When there is a procession, see 29.

80

Litany of the Blessed Virgin.

KYRIE eléison.
   Kyrie eléison.
Christe eléison.
Christe eléison.
Kyrie eléison.
Kyrie eléison.
Pater de cœlis Deus,
Miserére nobis.
Fili, Redémptor mundi Deus,
Miserére nobis.
Spíritus sancte Deus,
Miserére nobis.
Sancta Trínitas, unus Deus,
Miserére nobis.

LORD, have mercy.
   Lord, have mercy.
Christ, have mercy.
Christ, have mercy.
Lord, have mercy.
Lord, have mercy.
God the Father of heaven,
Have mercy on us.
God the Son, Redeemer of the world,
Have mercy on us.
God the Holy Ghost,
Have mercy on us.
Holy Trinity, one God,
Have mercy on us.

BENEDICTION. 115

Sancta María,	Holy Mary,
Sancta Dei Génitrix,	Holy Mother of God,
Sancta Virgo Vírginum,	Holy Virgin of virgins,
Mater Christi,	Mother of Christ,
Mater divínæ grátiæ,	Mother of divine grace,
Mater puríssima,	Mother most pure,
Mater castíssima,	Mother most chaste,
Mater invioláta,	Mother inviolate,
Mater intemeráta,	Mother undefiled,
Mater amábilis,	Mother most amiable,
Mater admirábilis,	Mother most admirable,
Mater Creatóris,	Mother of our Creator,
Mater Salvatóris,	Mother of our Saviour,
Virgo prudentíssima,	Virgin most prudent,
Virgo veneránda,	Virgin most venerable,
Virgo prædicánda,	Virgin most renowned,
Virgo potens,	Virgin most powerful,
Virgo clemens,	Virgin most merciful,
Virgo fidélis,	Virgin most faithful,
Spéculum justítiæ,	Mirror of justice,
Sedes sapiéntiæ,	Seat of wisdom,
Causa nostræ lætítiæ,	Cause of our joy,
Vas spirituále,	Spiritual vessel,
Vas honorábile,	Vessel of honour,
Vas insigne devotiónis,	Vessel of singular devotion,
Rosa mystica,	Mystical rose,
Turris Davídica,	Tower of David,
Turris ebúrnea,	Tower of ivory,
Domus aúrea,	House of gold,
Foéderis arca,	Ark of the covenant,
Jánua cœli,	Gate of heaven,
Stella matutína,	Morning star,
Salus infirmórum,	Health of the sick,
Refúgium peccatórum,	Refuge of sinners,
Consolátrix afflictórum,	Comforter of the afflicted,
Auxílium Christianórum,	Help of Christians,
Regína Angelórum,	Queen of Angels,
Regína Patriarchárum,	Queen of Patriarchs,
Regína Prophetárum,	Queen of Prophets,
Regína Apostolórum,	Queen of Apostles,

Ora pro nobis. — *Pray for us.*

Regína Martyrúm, — Queen of Martyrs,
Regína Confessórum, — Queen of Confessors,
Regína Vírgínum, — Queen of Virgins,
Regína Sanctórum ómnium, — Queen of all Saints,
Regína sine labe origináli concépta, — Queen conceived without original sin,
Regína sacratíssimi Rosárii, — Queen of the most holy Rosary,

Ora pro nobis. — *Pray for us.*

Agnus Dei, qui tollis peccáta mundi,
Parce nobis, Dómine.
Agnus Dei, qui tollis peccáta mundi,
Exáudi nos, Dómine.
Agnus Dei, qui tollis peccáta mundi,
Miserére nobis.
V. Ora pro nobis, sancta Dei Génitrix.
R. Ut digni efficiámur promissiónibus Christi.

Lamb of God, who takest away the sins of the world,
Spare us, O Lord.
Lamb of God, who takest away the sins of the world,
Graciously hear us, O Lord.
Lamb of God, who takest away the sins of the world,
Have mercy on us.
V. Pray for us, O holy Mother of God.
R. That we may be made worthy of the promises of Christ.

Then is said the prayer according to the season.

81

Tantum ergo Sacramentum.

TANTUM ergo Sacraméntum
Venerémur cérnui :
Et antíquum documéntum
Novo cedat rítui :
Præstet fides suppleméntum
Sénsuum deféctui.

Genitóri, Genitóque
Laus et jubilátio,

WHEREFORE this dread Host adoring, [due ;
Let us bend with reverence
Let the ancient rite departing
Yield and fade before the new ; [plying
Faith alone the proof supWhich the senses fail to view.

Unto the Sire and Son eternal
Praise and jubilation sing;

Salus, honor, virtus quoque Sit et benedíctio: Procedénti ab utróque Compar sit laudatio. Amen.

Saving health, immortal honour, [bring;] Glory, might and blessing And the same unto the Spirit Who from both doth equal spring. Amen.

V. Panem de cœlo præstitisti eis.
R. Omne delectamentum in se habentem.

V. Thou didst give them bread from heaven.
R. Containing in itself all sweetness.

In Paschal time, Alleluia.

OREMUS.

DEUS qui nobis sub Sacraménto mirábili, passiónis tuæ memóriam reliquísti: tríbue, quaésumus, ita nos córporis et sánguinis tui sacra mystéria venerári; ut redemptiónis tuæ fructum in nobis júgiter sentiámus. Qui vivis, et regnas, etc. Amen.

LET US PRAY.

O GOD, who, in this wonderful Sacrament, hast left us a memorial of thy passion; grant us, we beseech thee, so to venerate the sacred mysteries of thy body and blood, that we may ever feel within us the fruit of thy redemption. Who livest, etc. Amen.

82

Adoremus.

ADOREMUS in ætérnum sanctíssimum Sacraméntum.
Laudáte Dóminum, omnes gentes: * laudáte eum, omnes pópuli.
Quóniam confirmáta est super nos misericórdia ejus: * et véritas Dómini manet in ætérnum.
Glória Patri, etc.
Adorémus in ætérnum sanctíssimum Sacraméntum.

LET us adore for ever the Most Holy Sacrament.
O praise the Lord, all ye nations: praise him, all ye people.
For his mercy is confirmed upon us: and the truth of the Lord remaineth for ever.
Glory be to the Father, etc.
Let us adore for ever the Most Holy Sacrament.

83

Rhyme of St. Thomas Aquinas.

ADORO te devóte, latens Déitas,
    Quæ sub his figúris vere látitas :
Tibi se cor meum totum súbjicit,
Quia te contémplans totum déficit.
  Ave Jesu, pastor fidélium,
    Adaúge fidem ómnium in te credéntium.

Visus, gustus, tactus, in te fállitur,
Sed audítu solo tuto créditur :
Credo quidquid dixit Dei Fílius :
Nil hoc veritátis verbo vérius.
  Ave Jesu, etc.

In cruce latébat sola Déitas ;
At hic latet simul et humánitas :
Ambo tamen credens, atque cónfitens,
Peto quod petívit latro pœnitens.
  Ave Jesu, etc.

Plagas, sicut Thomas, non intúeor,
Deum tamen meum te confíteor.
Fac me tibi semper magis crédere,
In te spem habére, te dilígere.
  Ave Jesu, etc.

O memoriále mortis Dómini!
Panis vivus, vitam præstans hómini,
Præsta meæ menti de te vívere,
Et te illi semper dulce sápere.
  Ave Jesu, etc.

Pie Pelicáne, Jesu Dómine,
Me immúndum munda tuo sánguine,
Cujus una stilla salvum fácere
Totum mundum quit ab omni scélere :
  Ave Jesu, etc.

Jesu, quem velátum nunc aspício,
Oro fiat illud quod tam sítio :
Ut te reveláta cernens fácie,
Visu sim beatus tuæ glóriæ.
  Ave Jesu, etc.

83 *(Translation.)*

Adoro te devote, latens Deitas.

THEE prostrate I adore, the Deity that lies [eyes;
  Beneath these humble veils concealed from human
My heart doth wholly yield, subjected to thy sway,
For contemplating thee it wholly faints away.
  Hail, Jesus, hail ; do thou, good Shepherd of the sheep,
  Increase in all true hearts the faith they fondly keep.

The sight, the touch, the taste, in thee are here deceived ;
But by the ear alone this truth is safe believed ;
I hold whate'er the Son of God hath said to me ;
Than this blest word of truth no word can truer be.
    Hail, Jesus, hail ; etc.

Upon the cross thy Godhead only was concealed ;
But here thy manhood too doth lie as deeply veiled ;
And yet, in both these truths confessing my belief,
I pray as prayed to thee the poor repentant thief.
    Hail, Jesus, hail ; etc.

I see not with mine eyes thy wounds, as Thomas saw ;
Yet own thee for my God with equal love and awe ;
Oh grant me, that my faith may ever firmer be,
That all my hope and love may still repose in thee.
    Hail, Jesus, hail ; etc.

Memorial sweet, that shows the death of my dear Lord ;
Thou living bread, that life dost unto man afford ;
Oh grant, that this my soul may ever live on thee,
That thou mayest evermore its only sweetness be.
    Hail, Jesus, hail ; etc.

O mystic pelican, Jesu, my loving Lord,
Cleanse me of my defilements in thy blood adored,
Whereof one only drop, in thy sweet mercy spilt,
Would have the power to cleanse the world of all its guilt.
    Hail, Jesus, hail ; etc.

O Jesu, lying here concealed before mine eye,
I pray thou grant me that for which I ceaseless sigh,
To see the vision clear of thine unveilèd face,
Blest with the glories bright that fill thy dwelling-place.
    Hail, Jesus, hail ; etc.

84

Ave verum Corpus.

AVE verum Corpus natum
De María Vírgine,
Vere passum, immolátum
In cruce pro hómine.

Cujus latus perforátum
Unda fluxit et sánguine,
Esto nobis prægustátum
Mortis in exámine.

O clemens, O pie,
O dulcis Jesu, Fili Maríæ.

HAIL to thee! true Body, sprung
From the Virgin Mary's womb,
The same that on the cross was hung,
And bore for man the bitter doom.

Thou whose side was pierced, and flowed blood,
Both with water and with
Suffer us to taste of thee
In our life's last agony.

Son of Mary, Jesu blest,
Sweetest, gentlest, holiest!

85

Inviolata, intacta, et casta es.

INVIOLATA, intácta, et casta es, María,
Quæ es effecta fúlgida cœli porta.
O Mater alma, Christi charíssima,
Súscipe pia laudum præcónia.
Nostra ut pura péctora sint et córpora,
Te nunc flágitant devóta corda et ora.
Tua per precáta dulcísona,
Nobis concédas véniam per saécula.
O benígna, quæ sola inviolúta permansísti.

SPOTLESS and pure, Mary immaculate,
Now high exalted heaven's shining gate:
Christ's own beloved Mother, deign to take
Our hymnal praise for thy dear Son's sweet sake.
See, loving hearts and tongues entreat that we
In mind and body may be chaste like thee.
O gracious Queen, preserved alone from sin,
By thy sweet prayers forgiveness for us win.

86.

Te Deum laudamus.

TE Deum laudámus: * te Dóminum confitémur.

Te ætérnum Patrem * omnis terra venerátur.

Tibi omnes ángeli, * tibi cœli, et univérsæ potestátes:

Tibi Chérubim et Séraphim * incessábili voce proclámant:
Sanctus,
Sanctus,
Sanctus, * Dóminus Deus Sabaoth.

Pleni sunt cœli et terra * majestátis glóriæ tuæ.

Te gloriósus * Apostolórum chorus,

Te Prophetárum * laudábilis númerus,

Te Mártyrum candidátus * laudat exércitus.

Te per orbem terrárum * sancta confitétur Ecclésia.

Patrem * imménsæ majestátis.

Venerándum tuum verum * et únicum Fílium.

Sanctum quoque * Paráclitum Spíritum.

Tu Rex glóriæ, * Christe.

Tu Patris * sempitérnus es Fílius.

WE praise thee, O God; we acknowledge thee to be the Lord.

All the earth doth worship thee, the Father everlasting.

To thee all Angels cry aloud, the heavens and all the powers therein:

To thee Cherubim and Seraphim continually do cry:
Holy,
Holy,
Holy, Lord God of Sabaoth.

Heaven and earth are full of the majesty of thy glory.

The glorious choir of the Apostles praise thee.

The admirable company of the Prophets praise thee.

The white-robed army of Martyrs praise thee.

The Holy Church throughout all the world doth acknowledge thee.

The Father of an infinite majesty.

Thine adorable, true, and only Son.

Also the Holy Ghost, the Comforter.

Thou art the King of glory, O Christ.

Thou art the everlasting Son of the Father.

H

Tu ad liberándum suscep-
túrus hóminem, * non hor-
ruísti Vírginis úterum.

Tu devícto mortis acúleo,
* aperuísti credéntibus reg-
na cœlórum.

Tu ad déxteram Dei sedes,
* in glória Patris.

Judex créderis * esse ven-
túrus.

Here all kneel.

Te ergo quæsumus, tuis
fámulis súbveni, * quos pre-
tióso sánguine redemísti.

Ætérna fac cum sanctis
tuis * in glória numerári.

Salvum fac pópulum
tuum, Dómine, * et bénedic
hæreditáti tuæ.

Et rege eos, * et extólle
illos, usque in ætérnum.

Per síngulos dies * bene-
dícimus te.

Et laudámus nomen tuum
in sæculum, * et in sæculum
sæculi.

Dignáre, Dómine, die isto,
* sine peccáto nos custodíre.

Miserére nostri, Dómine :
* miserére nostri.

Fiat misericórdia tua, Dómine, super nos : * quemád-
modum sperávimus in te.

In te, Dómine, sperávi ; *
non confúndar in ætérnum.

When thou didst take
upon thee to deliver man,
thou didst not abhor the
Virgin's womb.

When thou hadst over-
come the sting of death, thou
didst open the kingdom of
heaven to all believers.

Thou sittest at the right
hand of God in the glory of
the Father.

We believe that thou shalt
come to be our Judge.

We pray thee, therefore,
help thy servants whom
thou hast redeemed with
thy precious blood.

Make them to be num-
bered with thy saints in
glory everlasting.

O Lord, save thy people,
and bless thine inheritance.

Govern them and lift
them up for ever.

Day by day we magnify
thee.

And we praise thy name
for ever; yea, for ever and
ever.

Vouchsafe, O Lord, this
day to keep us without sin.

O Lord, have mercy upon
us: have mercy upon us.

O Lord, let thy mercy be
shewed upon us, as we have
hoped in thee.

O Lord, in thee have I
hoped ; let me not be confounded for ever.

Litany of the Holy Name of Jesus.

87

KYRIE eléison.
Kyrie eléison.
Christe eléison.
Christe eléison.
Kyrie eléison.
Kyrie eléison.
Jesu audi nos.
Jesu exdudi nos.
Pater de cœlis Deus,
Miserere nobis.
Fili Redémptor mundi Deus,

Spíritus sancte Deus,
Sancta Trínitas, unus Deus,
Jesu, Fili Dei vivi,
Jesu, splendor Patris,

Jesu, candor lucis ætérnæ,

Jesu, Rex glóriæ,
Jesu, Sol justítiæ,
Jesu, Fili Mariæ Vírginis,
Jesu, amábilis,
Jesu, admirábilis,
Jesu, Deus fortis,
Jesu, Pater futúri saéculi,

Jesu, magni consílii Angele,
Jesu, potentíssime,
Jesu, patientíssime,
Jesu, obedientíssime,
Jesu, mitis et húmilis corde,

Jesu, amátor castitátis,
Jesu, amátor noster,
Jesu, Deus pacis,
Jesu, auctor vitæ,
Jesu, exémplar virtútum,
Jesu, zelátor animárum,
Jesu, Deus noster,

LORD, have mercy.
Lord, have mercy.
Christ, have mercy.
Christ, have mercy.
Lord, have mercy.
Lord, have mercy.
Jesus, hear us.
Jesus, graciously hear us.
God the Father of heaven,
Have mercy on us.
God the Son, Redeemer of the world,
God the Holy Ghost,
Holy Trinity, one God,
Jesus, Son of the living God,
Jesus, splendour of the Father,
Jesus, brightness of eternal light,
Jesus, King of Glory,
Jesus, Sun of justice,
Jesus, Son of the Virgin Mary,
Jesus, most amiable,
Jesus, most admirable,
Jesus, mighty God,
Jesus, Father of the world to come,
Jesus, Angel of great counsel,
Jesus, most powerful,
Jesus, most patient,
Jesus, most obedient,
Jesus, meek and humble of heart,
Jesus, lover of chastity,
Jesus, lover of us,
Jesus, God of peace,
Jesus, author of life,
Jesus, example of virtues,
Jesus, zealous lover of souls,
Jesus, our God,

Miserere nobis.

Have mercy on us.

LITANY OF THE HOLY NAME OF JESUS.

Jesu, refúgium nostrum,	Jesus, our refuge,
Jesu, Pater páuperum,	Jesus, Father of the poor,
Jesu, thesáurus fidélium,	Jesus, treasure of the faithful,
Jesu, bone Pastor,	Jesus, good Shepherd,
Jesu, lux vera,	Jesus, true Light,
Jesu, sapiéntia ætérna,	Jesus, Eternal Wisdom,
Jesu, bónitas infiníta,	Jesus, infinite goodness,
Jesu, via et vita nostra,	Jesus, our Way and our Life,
Jesu, gaúdium angelórum,	Jesus, joy of angels,
Jesu, Rex Patriarchárum,	Jesus, King of Patriarchs,
Jesu, Magister Apostolórum,	Jesus, Master of Apostles,
Jesu, Doctor Evangelistárum,	Jesus, Teacher of Evangelists,
Jesu, fortitúdo Mártyrum,	Jesus, strength of Martyrs,
Jesu, lumen Confessórum,	Jesus, light of Confessors,
Jesu, púritas Vírginum,	Jesus, purity of Virgins,
Jesu, coróna Sanctorum ómnium,	Jesus, crown of all Saints,

Miserere nobis. — *Have mercy upon us.*

Propítius esto,	Be merciful unto us,
Parce nobis, Jesu.	Spare us, O Jesus.
Propítius esto.	Be merciful unto us,
Exáudi nos, Jesu.	Graciously hear us, O Jesus.
Ab omni malo,	From all evil,
Ab omni peccáto,	From all sin,
Ab ira tua,	From thy wrath,
Ab insídiis diáboli,	From the snares of the devil,
A spíritu fornicatiónis,	From the spirit of uncleanness,
A morte perpétua,	From everlasting death,
A negléctu inspiratiónum tuárum,	From the neglect of thy inspirations,
Per mystérium sanctæ incarnatiónis tuæ,	Through the mystery of thy holy incarnation,
Per nativitátem tuam,	Through thy nativity,
Per infántiam tuam,	Through thine infancy,
Per diviníssimam vitam tuam,	Through thy most divine life,
Per labóres tuos,	Through thy labours,
Per agoníam et passiónem tuam,	Through thine agony and passion,
Per crucem et derelictiónem tuam,	Through thy cross and dereliction,
Per langúores tuos,	Through thy weariness and faintness,
Per mortem et sepultúram tuam,	Through thy death and burial,
Per resurrectiónem tuam,	Through thy resurrection,

Líbera nos, Jesu. — *Jesu, deliver us.*

LITANY OF THE HOLY NAME OF JESUS. 125

Per ascensiónem tuam,
Libera nos, Jesu.
Per gaúdia tua,
Libera nos, Jesu.
Per glóriam tuam,
Libera nos, Jesu.
Agnus Dei, qui tollis peccáta
mundi,
Parce nobis, Jesu.
Agnus Dei, qui tollis peccáta
mundi,
Exdudi nos, Jesu.
Agnus Dei, qui tollis peccáta
mundi,
Miserére nobis, Jesu.
Jesu, audi nos.
Jesu, exaudi nos.

OREMUS.

DOMINE Jesu Christe, qui
dixisti, 'Petite, et accipiétis;
quaérite, et inveniétis; pulsáte,
et aperiétur vobis;' quaésumus,
da nobis peténtibus divinissimi
tui amóris afféctum, ut te toto
corde, oré et ópere diligámus,
et a tua nunquam laude cessémus.

Sancti nóminis tui, Domine,
timórem páriter et amórem fac
nos habére perpétuum: quia
nunquam tua gubernatióne
destítuis, quos in solíditate tuæ
dilectiónis instituis. Per Dominum. Amen.

Through thine ascension,
Jesus, deliver us.
Through thy joys,
Jesus, deliver us.
Through thy glory,
Jesus, deliver us.
Lamb of God, who takest away
the sins of the world,
Spare us, O Jesus.
Lamb of God, who takest away
the sins of the world,
Graciously hear us, O Jesus.
Lamb of God, who takest away
the sins of the world,
Have mercy on us, O Jesus.
Jesus, hear us.
Jesus, graciously hear us.

LET US PRAY.

O LORD Jesus Christ, who
hast said, 'Ask, and ye shall
receive; seek, and ye shall
find; knock, and it shall be
opened unto you;' give, we
beseech thee, to us who ask,
the grace of thy most divine
love, that with all our heart,
words, and works, we may love
thee, and never cease to praise
thee.

Make us, O Lord, to have a
perpetual fear and love of thy
holy Name; for thou never
failest to govern those whom
thou dost solidly establish in
thy love. Through Jesus Christ
our Lord. Amen.

INDEX OF FIRST LINES.

ENGLISH HYMNS.

	No.
Again the time appointed see,	12
All hail, dear Conqueror, all hail,	22
All hail, great Conqueror, to thee,	49
Angels we have heard on high,	4
Creator-Spirit, all-divine,	26
Daily, daily, sing to Mary,	36
Dear Angel, ever at my side,	50
Dear Husband of Mary! dear Nurse of her Child,	52
Dear Maker of the starry skies,	2
Faith of our fathers! living still,	76
Flower of innocence, Saint Thomas,	58
God of mercy and compassion,	67
Hail, full of grace and purity,	47
Hail, glorious Saint Patrick,	57
Hail, holy Joseph, hail,	51
Hail, holy Mission, hail,	64
Hail, Jesus, hail, who for my sake,	34
Hail, Queen of heaven, the ocean star,	37
Hark, an awful voice is sounding,	1
Hark, hark, my soul, angelic songs are swelling,	73
Hark! the sound of the fight hath gone forth,	75
Have mercy on us, God most high,	28
Holy Ghost, come down upon thy children,	27
Holy Spirit, come and shine,	24
I worship thee, sweet Will of God,	69
It is no earthly summer's ray,	53

INDEX OF FIRST LINES.

	No.
Jesus is God; the solid earth,	71
Jesus, my God, behold at length the time,	66
Jesus, my Lord, my God, my all,	80
Jesus, the only thought of thee,	10
Joy of my heart, oh let me pay,	43
Like the dawning of the morning,	3
Look down, O Mother Mary,	38
Lord, by thy prayer in agony,	48
Mother of mercy, day by day,	39
My God, how wonderful thou art,	68
My God, I love thee, not because,	70
My Jesus, say, what wretch has dared,	18
Now are the days of humblest prayer,	13
O Christ, thou brightness of the day,	77
O Christ, thy guilty people spare,	61
O gracious Lord, Creator dear,	11
O Jesus, Jesus, dearest Lord,	72
O Mother, I could weep for mirth,	41
O Paradise, O Paradise,	74
O purest of creatures, sweet Mother, sweet Maid,	40
O spouse of Christ, on whom,	60
O thou, of all thy warriors Lord,	56
O'erwhelmed in depths of woe,	16
Oh, come and mourn with me awhile,	17
Oh, come to the merciful Saviour that calls you,	65
Oh, turn to Jesus, Mother, turn,	63
Once a very sinful woman,	59
Queen of the Holy Rosary,	46
See, amid the winter's snow,	7
Sing, sing, ye Angel bands,	42
Sound the mighty champion's praises,	54
Stars of glory, shine more brightly,	8
Sweet Saviour, bless us ere we go,	73
The clouds hang thick o'er Israel's camp,	45
The dawn was purpling o'er the sky,	20
This is the image of our Queen,	44

	No.
Thou who, hero-like, hast striven,	55
Thy sacred race, O Lord, is run,	23
To Christ, the Prince of peace,	32
To Jesus' Heart, all burning,	33
What a sea of tears and sorrow,	19
What beauteous sun-surpassing star,	9
When the Patriarch was returning,	31
Ye sons and daughters of the Lord,	21
Ye faithful, approach ye,	6

LATIN HYMNS, ETC.

	No.
Adeste, fideles,	5
Adoremus in æternum,	82
Adoro te devote, latens Deitas,	83
Ave maris stella,	35
Ave verum Corpus natum,	84
De profundis clamavi ad te, Domine,	62
Inviolata, intacta, et casta es, Maria,	85
Miserere mei, Deus,	14
O salutaris hostia,	79
Pange lingua gloriosi Corporis,	29
Stabat Mater dolorosa,	15
Tantum ergo sacramentum,	81
Te Deum laudamus,	86
Veni, Creator Spiritus,	25

LITANIES.

	No.
Of the Blessed Virgin,	80
Of the Holy Name of Jesus,	87

PRINTED BY BALLANTYNE, HANSON AND CO.
EDINBURGH AND LONDON.

www.ingramcontent.com/pod-product-compliance
Lightning Source LLC
Chambersburg PA
CBHW031343160426
43196CB00007B/730